ACCIDENTAL BRANDING

How Ordinary People Build Extraordinary Brands

DAVID VINJAMURI

WILEY

John Wiley & Sons, Inc.

Copyright © 2008 by David Vinjamuri. All rights reserved.

Published by John Wiley & Sons, Inc., Hoboken, New Jersey.
Published simultaneously in Canada.

No part of this publication may be reproduced, stored in a retrieval system, or transmitted in any form or by any means, electronic, mechanical, photocopying, recording, scanning, or otherwise, except as permitted under Section 107 or 108 of the 1976 United States Copyright Act, without either the prior written permission of the Publisher, or authorization through payment of the appropriate per-copy fee to the Copyright Clearance Center, Inc., 222 Rosewood Drive, Danvers, MA 01923, (978) 750-8400, fax (978) 646-8600, or on the web at www.copyright.com. Requests to the Publisher for permission should be addressed to the Permissions Department, John Wiley & Sons, Inc., 111 River Street, Hoboken, NJ 07030, (201) 748-6011, fax (201) 748-6008, or online at http://www.wiley.com/go/permissions.

Limit of Liability/Disclaimer of Warranty: While the publisher and author have used their best efforts in preparing this book, they make no representations or warranties with respect to the accuracy or completeness of the contents of this book and specifically disclaim any implied warranties of merchantability or fitness for a particular purpose. No warranty may be created or extended by sales representatives or written sales materials. The advice and strategies contained herein may not be suitable for your situation. You should consult with a professional where appropriate. Neither the publisher nor author shall be liable for any loss of profit or any other commercial damages, including but not limited to special, incidental, consequential, or other damages.

For general information on our other products and services or for technical support, please contact our Customer Care Department within the United States at (800) 762-2974, outside the United States at (317) 572-3993 or fax (317) 572-4002.

Wiley also publishes its books in a variety of electronic formats. Some content that appears in print may not be available in electronic books. For more information about Wiley products, visit our website at www.wiley.com.

ISBN 978-0-470-16506-5

Printed in the United States of America.

10 9 8 7 6 5 4 3 2

For Michelle

ACKNOWLEDGMENTS

This book would have been impossible without the support of Ryan Fischer-Harbage, whose heroic efforts while at Vigliano & Associates allowed this book to be published.

At John Wiley & Sons, Inc., Executive Editor Matt Holt, along with editor Shannon Vargo and editorial assistant Jessica Campilango, supported and encouraged me and offered valuable guidance during the writing process. Deirdre Silver kept the book on schedule when external events threatened. Christine Kim and Cynthia Shannon helped find the audience for the book, and the excellent production team led by Kim Nir with Erin Albright, and astoundingly detail-oriented copyediting by Tom Crippen, dramatically improved my sometimes-ungainly prose.

Aileen Dosé was invaluable in bringing the manuscript together, getting permissions, and keeping me on schedule for submission deadlines.

The team at Planned TV Arts—David Hahn, Alan Fox, and Dennelle Catlett—were impressively creative in finding ways to get attention for this book amongst the sea of other business books published this year.

Students from my NYU classes helped me form the idea behind *Accidental Branding*. Two of the chapters in this book were written after student papers revealed important details about the entrepreneurs. Thanks particularly to Gia Antonellis, Priscilla Nasrallah, and Mairi Brown for their contributions. Thanks also to Renee Harris, the excellent head of the Marketing Department at NYU SCPS.

Professionally, I am in debt to my friend Douglas Atkin as well as to the work of Seth Godin, Malcolm Gladwell, Al Ries, and Alex Wipperfurth, all of whom have improved the quality of thinking in the brand marketing discipline. Thanks also to Scott Williams and Dawn Kiernan who both gave me professional opportunities for ThirdWay Brand Trainers that made the writing of this book feasible and Paul Koulogeorge who has unswervingly helped the business grow.

During my marketing career, a few mentors helped me learn about brands and leadership, most notably Suzie Brown and Ann Simonds. On entrepreneurship, I have always looked to Stewart Greenfield, a longtime family friend and co-founder of Oak Investments, and my father, S.K. Vinjamuri, as great sources of wisdom.

Goldman Sachs technologist Walter Harris and English-professor-turned-star-investor Matt Greenfield were early readers of this manuscript and longtime supporters of my writing.

Finally, this book is for my wife, Michelle, who suffered through every last comma. With her help and support, I was able to finish *Accidental Branding* a week before our wedding day—much to our mutual relief.

Contents

FOREWORD
BY
CAROLYN KEPCHER

I will never forget the day that Donald Trump called me to tell me about a concept he was toying with for a reality series that would consist of an extended job interview for the Trump Organization. What I remember most is thinking that it was a terrible idea. But after spending five seasons sitting next to Donald on *The Apprentice* I learned a few things. I found that there is something special about entrepreneurs, and that the good ones learn to trust their instincts very early on. And I learned that while some people are born with the skills for entrepreneurial success, others can learn them by observation and practice.

Accidental Branding arrives at a great moment for me—just as I'm starting my own business, Carolyn & Co. David's easy-to-use advice has helped us position our brand with a simple, powerful message that speaks to our audience: a powerful network of career women who seek success in their careers and balance in their lives.

The lucid prose and vivid storytelling in *Accidental Branding* delighted me, and the tales of individual entrepreneurs—from John Peterman to Roxanne Quimby—were entertaining and easy to read.

These stories, and the distilled wisdom that David presents in the second chapter, "The Accidental Brand-Builder in You," aren't just for entrepreneurs, either. Learning how to stay faithful to your core customers and telling a story about your brand are skills that any corporate executive should master.

One other aspect of this exceptional book bears mentioning. By my count, four of the seven start-up stories in *Accidental Branding* feature female entrepreneurs. I cannot remember the last mainstream business book that did such a great job of featuring the contribution of female entrepreneurs to our society. These are stories worth reading and a book well worth passing on to a friend.

Carolyn Kepcher
CEO, Carolyn & Co., Inc.

INTRODUCTION

This book is about entrepreneurs and their extraordinary stories. My inspiration for this work came from a class project at New York University. I asked students to write about entrepreneurs who had created large consumer brands without any marketing training. One story that came out of this exercise seized my interest: that of Roxanne Quimby. She founded Burt's Bees, and there are a few magazine and newspaper articles written about her. My student had some inside information, however. Her best friend had gone to college with Quimby's daughter. My student wrote a story that was hard to believe—that Quimby was living in a tent in Maine with her 5-year-old twins when she met Burt, the beekeeper. That he picked her up while she was hitchhiking. And that she had built her empire—which she sold for $175 million in 2003—from an initial investment of around $400. It was a fantastic tale. It was also true, as I learned when I traveled to Maine to meet Quimby and learn about the even more extraordinary things she is doing today.

That story made me want to learn more about other entrepreneurs like Roxanne Quimby who had overcome overwhelming odds to build large and valuable consumer businesses. I soon found that there were numerous equally dramatic stories that had received little attention. Gary Erickson walked away from $60 million because he couldn't bear to leave behind the company he had built from scratch. Gert Boyle watched her husband die, then three days later she was forced to take over the company he ran. Her only training was 22 years as a housewife. Craig Newmark demoted himself from CEO to customer service rep in the company he founded. Eric Malka sold his only valuable possession, a snow-white BMW, to raise the money to open the first The Art of Shaving store with Myriam Zaoui. Julie Aigner-Clark dreamed up a product while nursing her first baby—and was selling it throughout the country by the time her second came along. John Peterman built up a fortune over more than a decade of hard work only to see it all come tumbling down. Then he started to build it all over again. With no disrespect to the thousands of great brands you see every day on television and in the aisles of your local supermarket, I think the stories of these entrepreneurs are worth reading.

The premise of this book is that there is something to learn from these seven different stories of brands that were founded by amateurs. I have reached some of my own conclusions, which I discuss in the second chapter, "The Accidental Brand-Builder in You," but please don't feel that you have to read sequentially. If there is a story you're interested in, jump right in. Even right now. My bet is that once you hear the stories of these amazing brands and the brave entrepreneurs behind them, you'll reach the same conclusions I have. I hope you enjoy the ride.

David Vinjamuri
New York, 2007

WHAT IS AN
ACCIDENTAL BRAND?

E ntrepreneurs fascinate me. They surrounded my childhood. There was always one at our dinner table. In school, I vividly remember the day Stew Leonard came to speak to my eighth grade class in the late 1970s. He talked about listening to customers and breaking rules. He actually made running a dairy store sound exciting. I spent summers in high school and college working for start-ups. I was a terrible computer programmer, but I loved the passion of the people working around me. Yet, when I left college, I took the safe route and went to work for a big strategic consulting firm. Then, after graduate school and a stint in corporate finance, I settled into a position as a consumer-products brand manager and followed that career, in one form or another, for over a decade.

I finally became an entrepreneur in 2003 and, soon after, started teaching marketing at New York University. My students were not MBAs but working professionals. Most came to marketing unexpectedly, having been promoted from other departments like sales or finance. Brand marketing, as it is practiced in major consumer corporations today, has its own language, practices and customs. It can be intimidating to an outsider and is a small, clubby world where most of us have heard of each other or at least know someone in common. The rapid developments in new media have shaken this up a little, but our business can still be a tough field to break into.

I taught a class on positioning and brand development in the summer of 2005 and for the final class project I asked each student to research and write about a successful consumer company that had been started by an entrepreneur who was not a trained marketer or an MBA. I thought that this would give my students some confidence and inspiration in their new marketing careers. I also believed that we could take some of these brands and compare them with brands launched by big consumer companies. The results surprised me. In paper after paper, I read about entrepreneurs who beat bigger companies with their tightly focused brands. And, in case after case, these entrepreneurs were doing some of the same things. These were not the things I had learned as a corporate marketer.

In truth, I had been having qualms about the "conventional wisdom" of marketing for a number of years. Reading Seth Godin's *Permission Marketing* in 2000 was a wakeup call for me. I had just left Coca-Cola to run a marketing group at the Internet advertising company DoubleClick. Godin questioned the entire model of marketing I was practicing at that point—marketing that was very much like a military assault and used the same terminology. The game in marketing was to make sure that anyone who might possibly be interested in your product heard your brand message at least three times. An intrusive message (we called it "breaking through the clutter") would increase the odds that the consumer would remember the brand. We measured success with memory-related tools like "Aided and Unaided Recall," a metric whose two categories refer, respectively, to recognizing a brand name when it's repeated to you and remembering the name on your own when all you're told is the type of product.

Godin, an entrepreneur himself, suggested that in an age of information on demand, this strategy was bound to fail. Consumers were being bombarded with too many commercial messages, and they were becoming frustrated with the intrusion into their lives. As people gained the ability to find what they were looking for (like news or stock quotes) without commercial interruption, they were starting to tune marketers out. Godin suggested that a relationship with a consumer is a value exchange, and that marketers need to be explicit about asking for permission to initiate the relationship as well as providing value to the consumer in order to get them interested in engaging with the brand. This would create a stronger, more lasting relationship with the brand.

I am embarrassed to say that I was still following my old marketing habits in 2003 when I was running marketing for a private-label company that hoped to launch a major branded product in the United States. I created a very traditional launch plan where millions of dollars would be spent to gain broadscale awareness of this new product. I did add some "viral marketing" elements to the mix, hired a strong PR agency, and tried to target "influencers" (people who influence the buying decisions of others, like doctors or journalists). But my marketing plan was still conventional, my wisdom outdated.

As the year rolled along, I began to have more doubts. There was a lot of data suggesting that television advertising just wasn't as effective as it had been 20 years before. I created a reading group within the company and our agencies and we read Malcolm Gladwell's *The Tipping Point*, which gave me even more qualms about the plan I had proposed. Gladwell suggested that ideas spread like viruses and that marketing messages take exactly the same route. This implied that all that television advertising wouldn't work if there wasn't some underlying message that people would really want to share with each other.

In 2005, a year after I had founded my own company to teach marketing to corporate brand managers, Bob Garfield wrote an article in *Advertising Age* that seemed to crystallize all of my doubts about conventional wisdom. Garfield quoted Shawn Burns, managing director of Wunderman, Paris, as saying, "There's been research that the real cost of obtaining 30 seconds of the consumer's attention is the same in 2005 as it was before the invention of television." What Garfield was saying was that the mass market—the ability to get to virtually everyone in America at the same time with a television commercial—was dead. Moreover, it wasn't exactly clear what was going to replace it. All in all, a pretty terrifying article for a marketing person to read and no doubt doubly frightful for advertising agency folks.

Just a couple of months later, I read Douglas Atkin's book, *The Culting of Brands*. Atkin talks about the deep relationship that certain brands develop with consumers and how these brands end up resembling cults—according to the strict sociological definition. I had the opportunity to interview Atkin for an article I was writing a couple of months after his book came out. We fell into a deep discussion about brands and the changes we were both seeing in the marketing community. We were both convinced that traditional marketing practices did not reflect the complexity of the brand experience. Atkin had done an excellent job of looking to the sociological model of cults to understand how consumers connect to brands. I wondered how else we could understand this connection.

The answer came to me as I was reading the student papers later that summer. The entrepreneurs they had chosen were not all of the same ones you will read about in this book (only two made the final cut—John Peterman and Roxanne Quimby), but they all had some important things in common. They were real people, mostly from very modest backgrounds. None of them had MBAs or a lot of special training. And although they were bright and incredibly motivated, these people were not geniuses. They were ordinary people.

Their brands, however, were not ordinary. Even from the original list of case studies from students, which included some Fortune 500 companies like Nike, Starbucks, and Apple, as well as brands created by entrepreneurs who were long deceased, I could tell that these brands were something special. Some of them had legions of fanatic followers. Others had assumed a cult standing and become cultural icons. It made sense that these entrepreneurs might know something that I didn't.

It also made sense for another reason. What I was looking at—in the 20-odd cases from students and the dozens of others that I subsequently investigated—was not just the results of a few individual efforts. It was the result of a Darwinian competition for resources that ruthlessly weeds out half of all start-ups. An even smaller number grow into large, profitable businesses. When you're talking about the kind of brands I was looking at—those with sales over $20 million that were 10 or more years old—the odds of success were even smaller. Thus, the companies that I actually investigated in depth represented hundreds or even thousands of others who failed. And there were a lot of similarities in these success stories. It's not just that people who start successful consumer brands have a lot of inherent traits in common—they also do some of the same things. Most important to me, I realized that this list of common practices was not the same list I'd been taught in my marketing classes at Harvard Business School, or while working for Johnson & Johnson or Coca-Cola. It was different stuff.

I ended up calling this book *Accidental Branding* because I realized that every brand that I wanted to write about started with some fortuitous accident. This does not mean that the founders didn't work hard and make a lot of smart decisions along the path to building huge businesses. But every story here starts with something unexpected happening, whether it is a cyclist realizing he can't eat his sixth consecutive energy bar because it just doesn't taste good (Gary Erickson of Clif Bar), a mother trying and failing to find videos with classical music, foreign language, and poetry for her baby (Julie Clark of Baby Einstein), or a hitchhiker getting picked up on the side of a road in Maine by a beekeeper who shares her values (Roxanne Quimby of Burt's Bees). I think the accident is important, because the foundation of all of these brands—what I'll call the brand architecture—was molded by that accident. These entrepreneurs all had a very clear set of values that they brought to the brand. Even though the actual products they sold would change over time for some of them, the values remained consistent. Moreover, these entrepreneurs were trying to solve their own problem. They were not listening to some focus group of consumers tell them what to do; they *were* the consumer. There has been a lot of controversy about the practice of following intuition and the value of making decisions from instinct. In my own career, I have seen and have made terrible decisions based on intuition. But after studying these entrepreneurs, I realized that most of those decisions came when I was very different from the consumers with whom I was trying to connect. These entrepreneurs could trust their instinct because they had retained the ability to think like real consumers. In fact, several of them got into trouble when they turned their businesses over to people without the same instincts.

    I ended up with a definition of an *Accidental Brand* that has three tests:

1. An individual who is not trained in marketing must create the brand.

2. This individual must experience the problem that the brand solves.
3. The individual must control the brand for at least 10 years.

By applying these three tests to my list, I was able to choose a set of brands that I felt I could learn from. Very early on, I also decided to limit my investigations to entrepreneurs that I could meet personally and who would spend time with me. This made the research a lot harder, but it allowed me to tell a more personal story about the brands. My thought was that because these entrepreneurs relied heavily on their personal tastes and instincts, I would see many echoes of their brand-building practices in their personal lives. This is exactly what I found.

THE ACCIDENTAL BRAND-BUILDER IN YOU

How do they do it? How do ordinary people create huge, valuable consumer brands? And more importantly, how do you know if you can be one of them? Let's start out with some cold, hard truth. All the entrepreneurs that I write about in this book, along with the dozens of others whose stories I reviewed to narrow the list down, were very, very lucky. Luck in and of itself would not have built businesses for them; there was also lots of sweat and planning and some great decision-making. But without luck, and especially good timing, there is a chance some of these folks would not have created huge businesses. Consider that a scientific study claiming that exposure to Mozart would make babies smarter came out a few weeks after the Baby Mozart video shipped—did this spur Baby Einstein's success? Hard to say. Would Burt's Bees have been as successful if it had not caught the wind of the environmental movement in its sails? We will never know.

On the other hand, it is hard to imagine that these accidental entrepreneurs would not have been successful even without the luck that made them hyper-successful. Several of them have proven it in their subsequent work. Gary Erickson now runs a successful wine business in addition to ClifBar. After Julie Clark sold Baby Einstein to Disney, she created The Safe Side with *America's Most Wanted* host John Walsh and was honored in the State of the Union address for her contributions to child safety. Roxanne Quimby will very likely become the best-known philanthropist in the history of the state of Maine, not because of her resources, but because she has brought her business acumen to land acquisition; just three years after selling Burt's Bees, she had put together the second-largest tract of environmentally protected land in the state.

So even if you are not lucky enough to put up your sail at the moment the winds of fortune are blowing, these entrepreneurs might just teach you something. The good news is that it's not about how rich your family is or how great a college you attended. There are no Ivy Leaguers in this book. Several of the entrepreneurs did not even graduate from college. You also don't need rich backers, provided you're willing to live hand-to-mouth while you are building the business. Gert Boyle almost lost her house and her mother's house when she took over Columbia Sportswear. Gary Erickson lived in a garage when he created ClifBar because he couldn't afford more than $300 a month in rent. Eric Malka sold his car to pay for the first The Art of Shaving store. Roxanne Quimby was living in a tent in Maine with her twins when she sold her first jar of honey.

RULE #1 – *DO* SWEAT THE SMALL STUFF

When I was a brand manager, I learned that the key to success in a corporation was to keep things moving and not to sweat the small stuff. Of course, when working on packaging or advertising, we were all supposed to be very careful, but outside of these big issues, our goal was to get things done on time. Perfectionists had a very difficult time in this environment.

Successful accidental brands are built just the opposite way. Every single person I interviewed for this book is a perfectionist. These entrepreneurs don't just pay attention to the big stuff; they obsessively sweat every detail. In fact, one of them was kind enough to correct punctuation in the chapter on his brand. Another sent me 14 pages of comments on his chapter—more than my editor. Interviewing their colleagues and coworkers, I hear much the same thing. Every piece of written communication that comes from the brand is scrutinized—whether it is a training manual, a flyer, or a new product announcement.

I learned from these entrepreneurs that it is just this attention to detail that makes these brands authentic. As consumers, we cue off very small things when we are interacting with brands. If I buy a new food processor, for instance, I don't just notice how well it shreds carrots or purees tomatoes. I want to see if it is easy to pour those pureed tomatoes from the work bowl of the food processor into a mixing bowl without spilling them. Then I will notice whether it's easy to clean the machine without getting the motor wet and whether I can stick that work bowl into my dishwasher. All of these small clues tell me if a serious cook designed the machine. If I have a problem, I expect to talk to someone who has actually used the food processor. This way I know that the machine I bought is not just a random product that the brand makes. I know they're experts.

Attention to detail is the best way to show consumers that you are an expert in your category. Walk into an American Girl store, for instance, and you'll see a company that gets all of the details right. They understand how girls interact with dolls, and they've created an obsessively consistent environment. Disney does the same thing at its theme parks and resorts. You'll see horses in the parades at Disney World, but you will never see any horse droppings. Why? Because Disney realizes that they're creating a fantasy world and that horses don't make a mess in a fantasy world. A lot of work goes into getting those small details right. Disney has networks of tunnels running under all of its properties so the guy with the shovel can inconspicuously disappear after he has—ahem—made the mess go away. Apple is another great example of a corporation that has learned to sweat the details. The iMac I am using to write this book has its entire case sheathed in a transparent layer of Lucite. Achieving this effect required creating a new manufacturing process and added expense. Apple (led by Steven Jobs, who is himself an accidental brand builder) could have easily saved cost and complexity by eliminating this design feature. Instead, they forged ahead because they wanted a product that was brilliantly designed down to the last detail. Look at an iPod next to any other MP3 music player and you'll see the difference in philosophy.

These last few examples are the exception among big corporations, but they're the norm for accidental brands. When Gary Erickson's company ClifBar launched Luna, Gary himself went into the baking kitchen to perfect the recipes for the new bars. John Peterman created catalogs that were so beautifully written and designed that the *New York Times* called him a "merchant poet." If you order from the J. Peterman catalog today, every single customer service rep is sitting no more than five steps away from the garment you might buy. J. Peterman reps can tell you exactly how each item is constructed because they've not only been trained on them but can hold the garment in their hands while they talk to you. Roxanne Quimby learned to keep bees, hand-dip candles, and formulate lip balm by hand before she sold the first jar.

The lesson here is simple. *Do* sweat the small stuff. Make sure you understand every way a consumer will interact with your brand, and choreograph all of those interactions. Don't compromise on a single element just to save cost, because the game you're really in is trying to get your consumers to reward you with a high profit margin. That's infinitely better than competing with other brands on price.

I must insert one cautionary note at this point. There is a big difference between being very detail-oriented and being a micromanager. If you plan to sell your company before it reaches 10 employees, as Julie Clark did, you may be able to personally approve everything that goes out the front door. If your brand grows larger, however, you will have to delegate. The key to successful delegation is picking people who are just as detail oriented as you are and training them to see things as you do. You have to give them your eye and pass along the DNA of the brand. Just like you, they should be actual consumers of the brand—they should experience the problem your brand solves, whether that is terribly chapped lips, a craving for a healthy snack, or the need to find a used trombone. If you don't do this, you'll find that it is terribly difficult to keep employees, because very few people like working for micromanagers. The best proof that the accidental brand builders in this book are not micromanagers is the high number of employees who stay to work with them in subsequent ventures. Both Roxanne Quimby and Julie Clark have new businesses exclusively run by former employees of their original companies. John Peterman was able to get employees back to the second version of a company that had gone *bankrupt*. That kind of loyalty can only be earned with good management.

RULE #2 – PICK A FIGHT

All of these accidental brands succeeded because they did more than create "me-too" products. They offered something genuinely new. In doing so, they took a stand against something—whether that was another brand or another way of doing things. Defining the "other," as Douglas Atkin calls it, or the ideology that the brand passionately disagrees with, helps define the brand. It also creates a strong creed that consumers can subscribe to. Creating a clearly stated value system is a key ingredient in building a loyal consumer base for a brand. Atkin uses the example of Apple and how it first demonized IBM (the famous "1984" commercial is a great example of this) and later Microsoft.

Every accidental brand in this book picked a fight with somebody. John Peterman launched a catalog with just one item on a page, no photography and florid descriptions of the products he sold. His brand, J. Peterman, took a strong stance against the crass utilitarianism of the rest of the catalog industry. Peterman understood that buying by mail order is a form of delayed gratification. J. Peterman substituted delirious anticipation for instant gratification and, in so doing, demonstrated that the former was the more precious commodity

Craig Newmark brought democracy to classified ads. He allowed people to exchange things with each other for free, only adding features that his users demanded. Even when it became clear that Craig could make a huge amount of money by running advertising on craigslist, he did not do so. And he limited fees to just two items: job listings and real estate ads. In both cases, craigslist fees were much lower than competing options. The site became one of the 10 largest on the Internet because it followed his simple but revolutionary philosophy: "Give people a break." For Craig, this meant making the site easy to use and making it free. By standing against the commercialization of exchange, Craig attracted loyal users.

Gary Erickson did not believe that an energy bar had to taste bad to work. While other bicyclists were thinking of the compact bars as "fuel," ClifBar aggressively created mobile food—bars that actually tasted good. Along the way, he realized that the whole foods he made the bars with were healthier too. Myriam Zaoui and Eric Malka allowed men to care for their skin without being feminized. They rejected the metrosexual movement while still advancing its aims. By bringing tradition to their The Art of Shaving stores in the form of dark woods, classic packaging, and barber chairs, they swam in a different direction from the rest of the industry, much to their good fortune.

Julie Aigner Clark created an unpolished, unslick video for babies. She rejected every convention of video production as well as every rule of selling to parents. Instead, Baby Einstein looked like a handcrafted work of art. Mothers could watch a video lovingly made by another mother, featuring her own children. The anti-corporate feeling of the video made the product special.

Gert Boyle rejected the conventional wisdom that outerwear companies had to either sell very expensive innovative products or cheap knockoffs. She used her legendary thriftiness and her willingness to engage customers directly to craft a product line that was tough, innovative, and inexpensive.

Roxanne Quimby didn't think that personal-care items needed to be made with chemicals and artificial ingredients to be effective. From lip balm to shampoo, she set out to prove that nature could coexist with industry. Every Burt's Bees product is the repudiation of most of the established brands that existed when Quimby launched her company.

Putting a stake in the ground and being willing to say, "I am right and those other brands are wrong" is also a good test for you. It will tell you if you have the passion you will need to create a great brand. Large corporations are very risk adverse, which is why you see so many variations of the same product on supermarket shelves. Do we really need 22 flavors of toothpaste or 14 kinds of dishwasher detergent? No, but that's what we get when the perceived risk of launching completely new brands is so high. Accidental brands take real risk by going against the status quo, but they reap rewards for doing so. They attract like-minded consumers who are loyal to the brand and willing to pay a premium for it.

RULE #3 – BE YOUR OWN CUSTOMER

Perhaps the biggest difference between accidental brand entrepreneurs and corporate marketers is that successful entrepreneurs are their own products' consumers. As a brand manager for Johnson & Johnson, I spent nearly half a decade working on feminine hygiene and personal care items. In that time, I never used a single brand that I was assigned to, not even the brand that I launched from scratch. The reasoning behind having me, a man, working on products used exclusively by women was that I could look at quantitative research to understand consumer opinions and listen to focus groups to understand their language. But when it came right down to it, I just didn't think like a woman. My reactions to choice were very different.

Accidental brands are almost always created when people solve their own problems. Julie Clark couldn't find a video she liked for her first baby, so she created one for her second child. Gary Erickson couldn't eat another PowerBar, so he created a bar that he could keep eating. John Peterman sold the coat he bought, wore and loved; then he sold other things he liked just as well. Solving your own problem makes you infinitely better at sweating the details, too. In fact, it is very hard to single out the important details of a product, its packaging, or its customer service unless you use it.

There is a final reason to be your own consumer: it gives you a better chance of finding the real business you should be in. Roxanne Quimby started out selling jars of honey and hand-dipped candles, but Burt's Bees didn't blossom until she created lip balm. Luna turned out to be a bigger business for ClifBar than the ClifBar itself. And Columbia Sportswear had to move all the way from selling formal hats to ski parkas before it found its niche. But one thing didn't change for any of these companies: the customer. Each brand had a clear philosophy shared by the core customers. Even if the first product they produced didn't turn out to be the "big idea," they were able to identify that idea when it came along, because they listened to their core customers.

RULE #4 – BE UNNATURALLY PERSISTENT

Most of the brands in this book took between 10 and 20 years to reach the $20 million mark. The first few years were often exceptionally, excruciatingly slow. John Peterman told me that there came a point where he considered getting out of J. Peterman—the same point he had folded up shop on a few earlier ventures. The business just didn't seem to be meeting his expectations at that moment. But because of his obligations to employees, customers, and creditors, Peterman was unable to quit. Only after he got through this period did he see the business jump ahead.

Seth Godin does a great job explaining this phenomenon in his book, *The Dip*. Of course, the real trick of surviving "The Dip" is not just identifying that your business has dipped, or even having the patience and persistence to keep going. The trick is to know *when* to keep going. I agree with Seth that you have to figure out if what you're doing is something you are good at, whether it makes sense for your customer, and whether you have the passion to sustain your effort. Unless you are extraordinarily lucky, though, your path to success will start slowly and involve a period of significant questioning and self-examination.

RULE #5 – BUILD A MYTH

I cannot overemphasize the importance of your founding myth to the success of your brand. Remember that consumers look for expertise, authenticity, and consistency in brands. I may only be hiking on a flat trail in the woods, but I want the same shoes that the best hikers wear on the John Muir or Appalachian trails. I'm more likely to believe this if I hear a story about a crazy hiker who designed her own shoes that all the other hikers started wearing because she never slipped.

The trick in building your founding myth is selecting the facts that you want to tell and deciding how best to share them. The word "mythology" comes from two Greek roots: *mythos*, meaning a narrative, and *logos*, meaning a speech or argument. Creating the mythology for your brand means that you have to understand both the narrative and how it will be spoken and shared. This is not as simple as it sounds. For instance, Myriam Zaoui and Eric Malka decided to found The Art of Shaving for several different reasons. When she lived in France, Myriam had always wanted to have her own spa. Eric and Myriam had agreed to open a little retail shop in Manhattan together. And Myriam had created pre-shave oil for Eric that allowed him to shave more comfortably without geting razor burn. All three narratives about The Art of Shaving are true. But the third creates a much more shareable story. Thus, when the company printed its own pamphlets, they told the story of Myriam creating the preshave oil for Eric and made it the company's founding myth. This is also the story you'll hear if you talk to their employees.

John Peterman also understood this. When he founded J. Peterman, he had been looking for an entrepreneurial win. He thought he could make some money by selling a coat that he was wearing that had drawn some compliments. But he had bought the coat because he thought it expressed his personality better than a trench coat did. By telling the last narrative eloquently, Peterman created a mythology around the coat that made him a mythic character. Peterman was careful to draw out that myth in his catalog and extend the mystery that it created. J. Peterman was so successful at creating a mythology that people would read the catalog for the stories it told.

You may not have a romantic founding story, but if you're an entrepreneur solving your own problem, you do have a story. By crafting this story carefully, you will make a better case for your business than any presentation or advertisement possibly could. You will know that your myth is a good one if it comes back to you from consumers.

RULE #6 – BE FAITHFUL

I grew up hearing the phrase "stick with the one that brought you to the dance" and thinking it was really about dancing (which caused some problems later). It makes good sense. Every day, I see brands get into trouble because they forget about the consumers that made them great. When a skateboarding brand stops supplying specialty products to skate shops so it can sell a few models in bigger numbers at chain stores, they have abandoned their core consumers. When an airline known for wide seats and great customer service starts charging for food and narrows those seats to "compete," I cringe. Why? Not because doing those things would always be bad in itself, but because it is a sign that the companies are just trying to grow revenue and have forgotten what made them special.

Every time Volvo forgets safety and decides to talk about how sexy, sleek, or sporty Volvos are, they walk away from the nervous parents who want the safest car for their kids—the parents that built the Volvo brand in the United States. When Wal-Mart has a runway show and starts advertising fashion apparel in *Glamour* magazine, they abandon the working families on which they built their business. When Orville Redenbacher comes back from the dead to promote his popcorn to hip kids, the brand betrays the consumers who remembered the real guy earnestly pitching better popcorn on television.

Stay true

What does this mean for you? Figure out who really supports you and keep listening to them. Don't be distracted by all of the other people who end up coming along for the ride as you become more successful. All of your success is based on the appeal that you established with their core consumers. When Phil Knight was selling shoes he designed with his track coach out of the trunk of his car, serious runners worshipped him. Now that Nike is a multibillion-dollar brand, it still listens to those serious runners, even though they are a tiny, tiny fraction of the brand sales. Why? Because Nike understands that the rest of us admire shoes that those serious runners wear because they're the best. (Notice that I did not say "professional runners" here—there's a difference.)

If you *are* the core customer, this task will be simpler for you. You just need to stay connected to the values that got you to start your business in the first place. Were you an overstressed road warrior? Make sure you still hang out with them. A corporate drone? Have a few over to dinner every week. Whatever it takes, be faithful to those people who made your brand great. If you don't, you will certainly regret it.

PUTTING IT ALL TOGETHER

I do not want to pretend that following these six simple rules will make you rich or guarantee the success of your next brand. But it is important to recognize that not all of these rules are today's conventional wisdom. I have sat in innumerable boardrooms and heard the phrase "We are limiting ourselves" or "We are giving away half of the market." Many businesspeople believe that if a product does not instantly appeal to everyone it is doomed to fail. Ignore them. Focus on creating a business that superbly meets the needs of a very few people. You'll know that you have succeeded when you have delighted, raving fans. That's the kind of base that Starbucks built—and the reason it was able to grow to the size it is now almost entirely without advertising.

Sweating the details is not conventional wisdom, either, and you are going to get a lot of resistance along the path. "Don't worry about whether it looks pretty—focus on whether it works," "Just keep perspective—everything is not advertising," and "Let's stay big-picture here" are all phrases that can kill your brand. A brilliant consumer experience—whether you are selling a product or a service (and, frankly, whether you are selling to consumers or to other businesses) is one where every step has been thought out to the last detail. It turns out that until you reach the last detail, consumers are just satisfied. When you actually nail the last detail they become loyal. Loyalty is your goal.

The last and hardest bit of unconventional wisdom to follow is to be persistent. In large corporations, brands have months to succeed.

A major launch can fail within the span of a calendar year. At one corporation I worked for, I was actually required to launch a new product at breakeven in the first year. I was successful, but I was lucky. If you follow the short-term approach, you won't be successful. For one thing, few of us (and even few corporations) have $100 million or more to invest in a new product launch, and that's the kind of money you need to ensure that *everyone* will hear about your product.

Frankly, that kind of business-building is not very satisfying either. For one thing, you can never afford to fail. Gary Erickson at ClifBar told me that the greatest single lesson he had learned in launching new products was to do it quickly and cheaply enough that he could afford to fail and keep innovating. Having the patience and persistence to keep launching new products after a big failure is what separates Gary from his corporate competitors.

It is very difficult for me to say this, but many people who follow this advice on persistence will nevertheless fail. Your business may have the wrong business model or cost structure, you might never really connect with your customers, or you might suffer a cash crisis or just have bad market timing. And being persistent will make these failures longer and more painful. But the possibility of success comes only through persistence. I once worked on a brand that had about 8 percent share nationally but over 30 percent share in Denver. "Why Denver?" I asked. It turns out that the brand had been launched with Denver as a test market. In Denver, the brand did all kinds of things from sampling to educational events to advertising in order to promote the brand. Initially, none of these activities paid out (produced a positive return on investment in the year they were run), and the brand was launched with a much smaller relative effort on a national level. But over 20 years later, the investment in Denver had proven to be the smart one. It is just that the brand didn't have patience to learn the right lesson.

Keep these rules in mind as you read the case studies ahead. I think you'll see that building your own brand can be a rewarding journey. And while you're on the way, make sure to patronize that little store in your neighborhood—you know, the one that everyone raves about but you've been hesitant to buy from because it's just a little more expensive than the big chain down the road?

The Storyteller:
John Peterman
(J. Peterman)

"This is a single-action Colt 45 Peacemaker, the gun that tamed the West," Peterman says, as he slides the long revolver out of his custom-made shoulder holster, flicks opens the cylinder, and loads .45 caliber bullets one by one. Then he hands me the gun. The sun hangs low in the Kentucky sky, pouring red light over Peterman's ranch on this midsummer's evening and making me squint as I inspect the Colt. It is a craftsman's piece that looks like it has been hammered out of a single hunk of iron. The handle is inlaid with smooth Bakelite, which is cool in my hand. It is heavy, much more so than it looks, and as I extend my arms to aim it I feel gravity pulling it groundward. I hold the gun carefully with two hands and sight down the barrel. Then, releasing my breath, I gently squeeze the trigger. Nothing happens.

"Just ease back the hammer when you're ready to fire," Peterman says calmly, as if he has not even noticed my failed attempt. I nod and slowly thumb the hammer toward me until it clicks into place. Then I line the shot up and pull the trigger again. This time the Colt jumps in my hand. It is loud, much louder than gunshots in the movies.

Peterman looks through binoculars at the can I'm aiming for, which is 40 feet away. "You're down and to the left. Don't flinch when you fire." I hadn't realized I'd flinched, but I notice it the next time, and the next. I continue firing through two reloads, shooting 18 rounds in total. My flinch gradually lessens, but although a stout poplar tree showers chips every time I fire, the can sitting in front of it does not seem to budge. Peterman is gracious with the limited supply of bullets. He gives himself a mere six shots. When we retrieve the coffee can, there are five holes in it. Peterman says, "Looks like you hit it a few times." He is being polite. I am pretty sure I've missed the can altogether and he's hit five of six.

The Peterman in question, the one I've come to central Kentucky to visit, is none other than *that* Peterman: John Peterman, the founder of the J. Peterman Company. He is the man who built his mail-order business to $70 million in sales and reinvented the catalog as we know it. His name is familiar to over 40 million Americans. In 1991, Holly Brubach in the Sunday *New York Times* called Peterman a "merchant poet." He is also famous because of the buffoonish caricature of him played by John O'Hurley on *Seinfeld* starting in 1995. Four years later, Peterman went spectacularly bankrupt at the height of his fame. And now he's back, quietly rebuilding the empire he lost.

Peterman has invited me to spend two days with him in Lexington, where I will interview employees at the J. Peterman Company (including his wife, Audrey), sit in on merchandising meetings, and see how the business runs. I am not sure he realizes that my central goal for engineering the entire trip is to visit the ranch I'm now standing on. After spending four hours interviewing Peterman in New York City a few weeks earlier, I've become convinced that the ranch will explain some of the mysteries of the myth he so successfully created. Even before *Seinfeld*, people were telling stories about J. Peterman. He was the world traveler who had fought in three wars, who hobnobbed with sheiks and maharajas, who looked equally comfortable at a state reception or tending a farm in Provence. Peterman's little *Owner's Manual* was a secret handshake for a certain set of people.

Along the way, the J. Peterman Company attracted some incredibly loyal customers, loyal enough to see their beloved business go bankrupt and still return as consumers two years later when Peterman revived it. In Lexington, I hope to answer a simple but elusive question—how did Peterman build this myth that motivated so many fanatic customers? And I have become convinced that the answer lies hidden at the Peterman ranch.

Peterman's cabin sits at one end of a 550-acre parcel of land that is farmed by his son Sean, who lives with his family at the opposite end. It is not Peterman's primary residence—a relatively modest home in Lexington serves that end—but his escape. The Kentucky bluegrass landscape, as viewed from the plank-wood porch of Peterman's custom-built two-story log cabin, is improbably lush. It looks like a Disney Imagineer or a movie colorist has retouched the view while saying, "Let's make the pasture a bit greener, shall we? The 200-year-old oak would look nicer there by the stream, wouldn't it?" But it's a real place and has some history to it. Famous Kentuckian Daniel Boone once lived nearby in Fort Boonesborough (southeast of present-day Lexington). On a Sunday afternoon in July 1776, his daughter Jemima was abducted by a war party of five Cherokee and Shawnee warriors while canoeing on the Kentucky River with friends Elizabeth and Frances Callaway. Boone tracked the braves for three days and ambushed them at a ford in the Licking River, bringing the three children home safely. The Licking River runs through Peterman's spread, and Peterman and his son regularly dig up arrowheads in the fields when they plow. The whole farm was later part of a larger spread that was owned by a Confederate colonel and had a working hospital on it during the Civil War.

As we're climbing the stairs back to the porch of the cabin after shooting the Colt, I remark to Peterman that I've enjoyed it. And I have. Regardless of my political beliefs and any lack of inclination to shoot at fuzzy animals, there is something primal and powerful about firing a gun. It gives me a surge of adrenaline, like stepping on the accelerator of a Mustang or starting the downward descent on an old wooden roller coaster. Peterman stops and cocks his head for a moment. Then he says, "Have you ever fired a shotgun?"

I hesitate for a moment because I have a complicated relationship with shotguns, dating back to 1973 when I was briefly placed in the hands of an ex-Marine just returned from Vietnam by the Big Brothers organization. He apparently thought firing off 12-gauge shotguns in a junkyard was a great afternoon for a nine-year-old. The guns bruised and scared me but no less than my Big Brother, who was eventually replaced by a saner man. But I have not handled a shotgun since and the thought makes me slightly queasy.

Taking my uncertain smile for assent, Peterman disappears into the cabin and comes out holding a short-barreled shotgun. "This is a coach gun—the same one they used to protect stage coaches a hundred years ago. It's a sawed-off, double-barreled gun with exposed hammers." He shows me how to break the gun open and load it. The barrel is short, just the length of my forearm, and a leather strap runs end to end—from just under the tip of the barrel to the end of the solid walnut stock. It is a beautiful piece that manages to simultaneously look graceful and deadly, like the Colt. Peterman hands me the shotgun.

I remember to pull the gunstock tight against my shoulder, but I'm worried about hitting my nose against the barrel when the gun recoils, so I don't get too close. When I squeeze the trigger, the little gun pushes back against me and I miss the little plastic ball I'm shooting at. But, for an adult, the recoil is not as frightful as I remember, so I bear down a little, look down the barrel, and hit the ball with the next two shots and the following two after that. My brain knows that hitting a ball that is not moving from 30 feet away with a shotgun is not much of an accomplishment, but I still feel color in my cheeks. Peterman is building me up, but knowing this doesn't make me feel less happy.

"You'd better stop. I can't leave myself without any ammunition," he warns me, and I realize that this gun, like everything else in Peterman's universe, has a functional as well as an aesthetic purpose. It may be a piece of artwork, it may remind me of Clint Eastwood Westerns and tumbleweeds, but the shotgun also protects Peterman's dog and calves from coyotes and his cabin from intruders. This is the first rule in the Peterman myth—everything has to have both romance (Peterman calls it "factual romance" because it is romance based on a real history) and function. To enrich your life, an item needs both a story and a purpose, and the purpose has to be suited to the world you want to create for yourself.

Peterman's rise to fame started with an unplanned excursion. In 1986, having left a long stretch as a salesman for General Foods and a shorter one with a plant food manufacturer, Peterman was working as a specialty-foods sales consultant. He was on a trip out West and decided to hop a flight to Wyoming. Peterman went to Jackson Hole, which was known but not yet discovered. It had a feeling Peterman liked: raw and authentic. "Elk still have the right of way in Jackson," he says. He stopped into a local outfitter's shop and spotted a cowboy duster. This is a long white canvas coat that is meant to protect a mounted cowboy from wind, rain, dust, thorns, and other hazards of the open range. Peterman wore it out of the shop and kept right on wearing it for the next several months. He attracted a lot of attention. The jacket seemed to predispose people toward him. It said he was not afraid to be different and suggested that he might be interesting to know—a real character. The pivotal moment for Peterman came when Donald Staley—an advertising copywriter and close friend of Peterman's—said to him, "You know, Peterman, I like you better when you wear that coat."

The longer Peterman wore the duster, the more frequently he was asked about where he found it. He was already dabbling in several entrepreneurial ventures at the time and thought he could make a few thousand bucks by selling the coat through newspaper ads. Working with Staley, he took out an ad in the Lexington (Ky.) *Herald-Leader* and sold exactly one coat. To his accountant's secretary. But the second ad did better, as did going to craft shows to sell the coats directly, which netted Peterman and Staley $2,000 in February and $5,000 in March. In April 1987, Peterman took a chance on a national ad in the *New Yorker*:

> **The J. Peterman Coat.**
> **$170**
> **Protection against the winds of Wyoming, the blizzards of Wall Street. Classic horseman's duster protects you, your rump, your saddle, and your legs down to the ankles. Because it's cut very long to do the job it's unintentionally very flattering, with or without a horse. High-count natural cotton canvas. Lightweight waterproof lining. Nine pockets. The first time people see you wearing The J. Peterman Coat, they're going to say, "Where did you get it? I've always wanted one of those." Tell them somewhere east of Laramie.**

The April ad helped Peterman sell $15,000 that month. Then the business started to grow exponentially. All in all, the new company, which initially consisted of just Peterman, Staley, and Peterman's wife, Audrey, took in $580,000 that year, all in dusters. With this success, Peterman began to expand. One day near the end of the year, he saw a picture of a colonial shirt in a history magazine. He admired the simple cut of the collarless shirt and decided to produce it, christening it the "J. Peterman Shirt." Then Peterman told Staley, who harrumphed and said, "Ah, yes. 99 percent Thomas Jefferson, 1 percent J. Peterman." That line eventually made its way into the ad copy for the shirt. Peterman also found a mailman's bag that he reworked to function as a carryall. Both items sold well.

The success of the coat, shirt, and bag, and the tricky economics of single-item newspaper ads, led Peterman and Staley to conclude that they needed to have a catalog—something they could send to customers to capture follow-up business. But neither man had any experience with direct mail and, in their haste, they neglected to call in any experts. The catalog they designed was unlike any other existing catalog, and more than anything it was responsible for creating the myth of J. Peterman.

To begin with, the J. Peterman catalog was not a catalog at all. It was an *Owner's Manual*, and at $5\frac{1}{2}$ inches $\times$ $10\frac{1}{2}$ inches it was an unusual size as well. Calling it the *Owner's Manual* might have made sense to the consumer who had just taken possession of a J. Peterman Coat or shirt, but it was certainly a novelty for those who found one in their mailbox as Peterman began to purchase lists and undertake direct mailings.

Unlike most catalogs, the *Owner's Manual* had no photography. Instead, artist Bob Hagel illustrated each product with a sketch. Each page featured just one product instead of the four to five per page in an ordinary catalog. And the product descriptions told stories about the items. The copy for a bone-handled badger shaving brush, for instance, said:

> **Jermyn St., and nearby Old Bond St., are exactly what you (if you were an Englishman) might dream about, if you unexpectedly found yourself pinned beneath an avalanche of boulders at the bottom of the Min Gorge in China. Waiting to be rescued, your mind might turn to the cool hushed perfection of all the tiny elegant shops along certain London streets, shops where clerks read your mind, anticipate your wishes, bringing forth soothing potions, perfectly fitted shoes, impeccable linen suits, cartridge belts, shooting gloves, rare oriental carpets, cucumber sandwiches, leather-bound first editions, coin-silver snuff boxes . . .**
>
> **Dreaming of these things, no doubt, has kept many an Englishman sane.**

J. Peterman was not the first company ever to offer unusual items or to bring things back from the past. But Peterman was uniquely gifted at striking the right compromise between romance and hard sense, balancing a stubborn practicality alongside a yearning for the quality that has been lost in our disposable society. When others tried to copy this, they often fell flat. Even the great Ralph Lauren never mastered the skill as well as Peterman, though he trod a similar path. Peterman's secret was that he was obsessive about the copy even when he did not write it himself. At the outset, these stories were the collaborative product of Don Staley and Peterman. Later a team of copywriters produced them. But Peterman had an uncanny ear for the voice of the brand, and he would personally approve every line of copy.

Peterman understood from the beginning that there would always be a gap between J. Peterman the brand and Peterman the individual. When he talks about the brand, Peterman calls J. Peterman "he"—as if the brand were a real person, just not himself. Peterman always intuitively knew that the brand character he was creating would assume proportions that Peterman as a flesh-and-blood person could never live up to. He has an artist's sense about how to nourish and build that character. He is quick to point out that J. Peterman is the work of many hands, yet there is something fundamental in the J. Peterman character that stems from Peterman's personality and his unique belief system. And though it has matured with age, his value system comes directly from his childhood.

[handwritten margin note: Sense of "myth"]

Peterman was born in 1941 to Charles Peterman, a plain, hard-working man who had risen from the mailroom to become a loan officer with Irving Trust. In one way, however, Charles Peterman was extraordinary. In 1938, three years before Peterman was born, Charles moved the family from Manhattan to Van Houten Fields, an agrarian commune in West Nyack, New York. It was a planned community created by a group purchase of an Old Dutch farm in the Hudson Valley. The modest working people who bought into this community had to build their own houses and agreed to grow a portion of their own food, making necessity a virtue.

In a stroke, this changed Peterman's childhood from the potentially urban future he might have faced to a somewhat idyllic rural existence (even though his father continued to commute into Manhattan). The third of four children, Peterman enjoyed a childhood full of the stuff of a Garrison Keillor yarn. He spent summers stealing rides from un-harnessed horses in a nearby pasture, jumping in a swimming hole at an old quarry, and playing cowboys and Indians. The long summers gave him ample time to indulge and develop his imagination. He learned to create and inhabit worlds that were lost in time and places that never existed at all.

The commune also taught Peterman the value of hard work. He grew up gardening and tending chickens, and he still does a great deal of manual labor on his cabin and his son's farm. In the two days I spend wandering around the warehouse and headquarters of The J. Peterman Company, the one comment I repeatedly hear from employees at all levels is how willing Peterman is to get his hands dirty and pitch in at any task. As a management tool, this trait is invaluable—Peterman will never ask anyone who works for him to do something he will not do himself, and he unloads pallets often enough to prove it. Peterman's model for his business is the family. He is more patriarch than CEO, and this may explain the loyalty of his employees, some of whom left better-paying jobs to rejoin him at the resurrected J. Peterman Company.

Peterman stows the guns and gives me a tour of the cabin. It is an authentic log cabin, but it was built to Peterman's design specifications by Hearthstone, a modern cabin maker based in Tennessee. The dovetailed spruce logs that form the shell of the house are sealed with mortar. The floor, which Peterman laid down by hand, is made of 80-year-old yellow pine salvaged from a warehouse. The beams supporting the floors are fitted mortise and tenon, as are the beams for the exposed staircase leading to the second floor. The floor plan is open, and the entire first floor of the cabin is a single great room of 1,000 square feet. At one end, a leather sofa that Peterman designed for his furniture line (the sofa is called the Faubourg, for the Rue du Faubourg St. Antoine in Paris) faces a stone Rumford fireplace with a wood-burning stove for efficient heat distribution. The other half of the room is split between an open kitchen and a dining area. A large bathroom with a huge, freestanding cast-iron tub and separate shower completes the first floor. The second floor has two large bedrooms. There is also a basement made entirely of fieldstone from the farm, which provides storage and houses the 500-bottle wine cellar that Peterman is in the midst of creating. The entrepreneur is converting a bread rack to hold wine bottles, and from France he has imported a riddling rack (used to make champagne) that he conscripts me to drag from his pickup into the cabin.

The cabin is furnished with many authentic pieces and replicas, but Peterman has a very hard-nosed approach to the items he surrounds himself with. "I want romance, but it has to be <u>factual</u> <u>romance</u>. Just because something is older does not necessarily mean it is better." As we walk out onto the hardwood deck that faces out over the Peterman spread, he points down to a brick patio that he has constructed with 200-year-old bricks from a friend's old farmhouse. The bricks, which have done fine as the floor for the basement, have begun to crumble after just a year as an outdoor patio and this annoys Peterman. It's the kind of misstep that he carefully avoids in the *Owner's Manual.* Peterman loves old, authentic, original things with history, but they must function better than their modern counterparts. Inside the cabin, there are unabashed nods to modern luxury, like the Bosch dishwasher and a contemporary reproduction of a nineteenth-century giant flowerhead faucet in the oversized shower stall. Peterman has handpicked 11 pieces of the furniture from the collection that sold in the retail stores, among them a French Country table and a Vacqueyras wine table, along with the Faubourg Sofa and Chair.

We have just enough time to take a quick walk before dinner and Peterman wants to show me his new vineyard. He kneels down and scoops up a handful of the rich Kentucky earth and explains the science of winemaking as the soil slides between his fingers: "The more organic matter you have in soil, the better it is. Then there's clay—and that dries out and gets very hard and powdery and it won't absorb water, so you have to mix sand with it and some organic matter. We brought 26 tons of sand here last year." I ask him about the varieties he is growing and he points and says, "Those are cabernet franc and these are baco pinot—a variety of pinot noir. ... It's a big experiment," he admits. "Grapes will grow most anywhere, but I have no idea what these will taste like in this earth." When I press him for his reasons for dabbling in winemaking, he finally confesses the true purpose, "I really wanted to be able to look out from the porch [of the cabin] and see a vineyard." Then he smiles, wistfully. "But this is a lot of work. I'm like a plantation owner without any labor."

It wasn't always the case. A dozen years earlier, in 1994—the year that Peterman bought the land for his cabin—the J. Peterman Company was at its peak. Sales had grown exponentially to $62 million and the company had an enviable and loyal customer base. The clients were well heeled and connected. Peterman remembers personally giving advice to a number of them, including *Top Gun* star Kelly McGillis. The *Owner's Manual* had become a sort of secret handshake among a certain set of moneyed people. A group of friends on Martha's Vineyard took the *Owner's Manual* to the beach in the evening and read aloud from it, introducing the Geometry Skirt woman to the Paris Raincoat man. Knowing about the Peterman catalog was a sign of an advanced shopper, someone who was more discerning and reached farther than The Gap or J. Crew.

The secret world of J. Peterman ended on April 18, 1995. On that evening, *Seinfeld* introduced a new character. On that episode, Jerry Seinfeld's friend Elaine Bennis is on a rainy sidewalk, distracted and depressed, when she literally runs into a tall, distinguished, silver-haired gentleman:

ELAINE: *Oh, oh God, I'm so sorry. I don't even know where I'm going.*
MAN: *That's the best way to get somewhere you've never been.*
ELAINE: *Yeah, I suppose that's true.*
MAN: *Have you been crying?*
ELAINE: *Yeah, you see, this woman, this manicurist . . .*
MAN: *Oh no no. It doesn't matter why. That's a very nice jacket.*
ELAINE: *(cheering up at the attention): Oh, thanks.*
MAN: *Very soft. Huge button flaps. Cargo pockets. Drawstring waist. Deep bi-swing vents in the back. Perfect for jumping into a gondola.*
ELAINE: *How do you know all that?*
MAN: *That's my coat.*
ELAINE: *You mean . . .*
MAN: *Yes. I'm J. Peterman.*

Suddenly, J. Peterman was known by more than a fifth of all adults in the United States. The little cult company became a mainstream phenomenon and Peterman himself became a minor celebrity. *[handwritten: A case of bad advertising]* Peterman believes that Seinfeld was very, very bad for the company. John O'Hurley—the actor who played Peterman on Seinfeld—agrees. "It was a strange circumstance where the parody becomes larger than the company," he says.

On the face of it, it's hard to understand why *Seinfeld* would pose such a problem for J. Peterman. *Seinfeld* made lots of things easier for the company. It made investors more willing to consider a retail expansion, gave more cachet to holding a job at J. Peterman, and made hiring easier for the company. It eventually landed Peterman CNN coverage and a shot at a network television show of his own. But *Seinfeld* put J. Peterman in the spotlight long before the organization was ready. The publicity instantly transformed the family-run Lexington enterprise from a scrappy bunch of outsiders to an industry model and consumer buzzword. It also made J. Peterman a mainstream retailer, a role Peterman was not ready to take on. And the *Owner's Manual* went from being a well-kept secret to being no secret at all. By outing the brand to a wider audience, Seinfeld actually caused J. Peterman to lose some of its cachet. The brand is still struggling to get back into the closet.

Another problematic effect of the *Seinfeld* exposure was to confuse the J. Peterman myth for potential customers. The brand personality that Peterman, Staley, and their small company had so painstakingly created bit by bit over nearly a decade was satirized for a public largely unaware of it to begin with. For insiders who understood J. Peterman and valued the products, the John O'Hurley character may have been amusing. O'Hurley played Peterman to the hilt with a magnificent, overblown weepy romanticism and congenial thickness. When O'Hurley was called in for an audition, he at first turned down what looked to be a brief role and then reconsidered when the pilot he was working on was scuttled. When he came in for the interview, he was handed the J. Peterman catalog and asked to create the character behind the catalog. "I conceived of a character that sounded like a bad Charles Kuralt in a 1940s radio drama."

The writers made the *Seinfeld* version of J. Peterman a neat piece of social satire by parodying the late-stage materialism that allows J. Peterman to persuade consumers to attach emotional meaning to clothing and everyday objects. And the writing of the J. Peterman character was affectionate—both Jerry Seinfeld and Larry David were J. Peterman customers before the brand was written into the series script.

But consumers who had never heard of J. Peterman before *Seinfeld* saw something entirely different. For them, O'Hurley's version of J. Peterman was a preening buffoon—straight slapstick without the irony. The brand looked ostentatious and silly, and although the exposure turned the real Peterman into a celebrity, it did not give consumers strong reasons to become J. Peterman customers. In this way, the *Seinfeld* character became a joke at J. Peterman's expense.

The worst effect of *Seinfeld* on J. Peterman, however, may have been the strategy shift that it forced on the company. More than any single other factor, the exposure on *Seinfeld* made a huge retail expansion attractive to the company and attractive for investors. Unfortunately for Peterman and his crew, the exposure on *Seinfeld* neatly coincided with a rough patch for direct marketers.

A rapidly expanding business creates significant cash flow problems in the direct mail industry. Both advertising and inventory expenses are incurred before the first penny of profit is realized. Suppliers are small and unable to extend much credit, so the catalog retailer must pay before he knows whether the catalog will even cover its variable cash costs. If the business is expanding at 40 percent or more a year, as J. Peterman was throughout the late 1980s and early '90s, it is perpetually in debt. The profit from each cycle of the *Owner's Manual* was never enough to pay for the expanding inventory and advertising costs of the next season. Moreover, the business was extremely vulnerable to a recession. Just such a downturn arrived in 1995. It was a very bad year for the entire industry, and, in spite of the *Seinfeld* exposure, J. Peterman lost money.

In 1996, Peterman turned to help from Arnie Cohen, the former president of J. Crew, when he ran into an inventory situation that threatened to starve J. Peterman of cash. Peterman and Cohen had met several years earlier when Peterman had visited J. Crew. Unsurprisingly, given his background, Cohen's prescription for J. Peterman was a venture capital–funded retail expansion. Cohen agreed to help Peterman raise funding and then to come in-house as president of J. Peterman.

Peterman calls the next three years his personal "ride at the helm of the *Titanic*." He spent the first half of 1997 working with Cohen to draft a retail plan and close funding for it. The Bank of Montreal, Nesbitt Burns Equity Partners and Brand Equity Ventures put up $11 million to stabilize the company and fund the retail expansion. The plan was to grow the company to a minimum of 70 retail stores and $250 million in revenues within five years. Then Peterman and Cohen started working on the flagship store and quickly settled on a location in Manhattan at Grand Central Terminal. During this time he was increasingly disengaged from the *Owner's Manual* and the core business.

The advisability of the retail expansion is a difficult issue for Peterman. In 1997, Peterman was desperate to grow J. Peterman and he felt that he had reached the limit to which his catalog business could aspire. He had tried launching a hard-goods catalog called *Booty, Spoils, and Plunder,* which featured exotic items like a motorcycle with a sidecar, but it never made money. On the other hand, the one existing J. Peterman retail store (in the company's hometown of Lexington, Kentucky) had been profitable nearly since Peterman had opened it in 1992. It was his own personal laboratory, an experiment that he was immensely fond of. His metaphor for the store was his grandmother's barn, a place he had explored as a child. He wrote about his experience in the *Owner's Manual,* in the description for a piece of luggage:

> **It's time to go to the secret barn . . .**
>
> **Look·. . . there under that huge pile of saddles and hats . . . it seems to be the hood of a car . . . It's the 12-cylinder Packard convertible someone (Emily?) once drove across the country. The doors are locked.**
>
> **. . . but inside, the car seems to be stuffed with old clocks, framed oil paintings, a leopard skin, books, boots, old brass fishing reels, stamp albums . . .**
>
> **You can't take it all in. At the other end of the barn you notice a marble table, a beautiful slim-wheeled two-seat carriage, a stack of a dozen carved chairs, a leather trunk . . . it's all too much at once.**

There is an obvious parallel between Peterman's retail dreams and those of Ralph Lauren. The Ralph Lauren flagship store, which opened in 1986, was also something like grandmother's barn. It was built to be a complete environment to showcase the brand and included lots of big and expensive items that were ostensibly for sale but which Lauren knew were more important for atmosphere than for revenue. In this context, Peterman is Ralph Lauren's eccentric, globe-trotting uncle. The Ralph Lauren store might have some heartbreakingly exquisite tooled leather wardrobes or a fantastic carved hardwood four-poster bed, but you weren't going to find English House of Commons silver for sale or the bronze statue of Babe Ruth from the old Yankee Stadium.

Ralph Lauren had a singular motivation in opening the flagship store. His lines were already sold at retail, but he felt he had limited control of the retail environment. He was not happy with the merchandising of his line—retailers tended to cherry-pick the collection and he had great difficulty taking some of the risks he thought were necessary for his business to succeed. For Ralph Lauren to succeed, he needed to prove to retailers that creating a special environment for his products would strengthen the brand and dramatically increase sales. The flagship store was risky but successful and became a model for subsequent manufacturers like Nike and Apple who were also struggling to present their brand face directly to the world in order to change the balance of power with retailers.

Peterman's motives for retail expansion were different, much closer—unfortunately—to those of direct marketer Gateway's. He felt that he had tapped out the potential of the *Owner's Manual.* His company had a significant cash flow issue that could only be solved by an injection of capital. And retail expansion was the best strategy to sell to venture capitalists, who expected significant returns on their money. Most of all, the retail store gave Peterman the opportunity to do what he loved doing—to build and tinker with environments.

But retail expansion presented a major challenge for the J. Peterman brand. The hallmark of the brand was that it was an "insider brand." This status was badly damaged by the exposure on *Seinfeld,* but the retail expansion threatened to kill it entirely. What good would it be to tell your friends about this amazing little catalog you get every month if the company has a store in Grand Central Terminal and in 70 other locations around the United States?

Still, elements of the expansion were successful. Sales at the J. Peterman retail stores in New York and Seattle averaged $800 per square foot, twice the retail industry average. There is some evidence that consumers were interested in the retail concept and they responded with purchases. But the rest of the news was bad. When Peterman turned daily operations over to Cohen in mid-1997, the company almost immediately missed catalog projections and faced several unexpected cash crises. Even with the cash infusion from new investors, the J. Peterman Company was operating on a razor-thin cash margin. Disappointing sales results combined with questionable inventory management brought the company to the point of illiquidity several times. Moreover, there was a strong cultural gap between Peterman the entrepreneur and Cohen the corporate CEO. On one trip to Los Angeles, Peterman and Audrey found themselves riding in coach while one of Cohen's handpicked J. Peterman managers sipped cognac in first class.

Within 18 months of closing the expansion deal and installing Cohen as COO, Peterman was forced to start firing longtime employees. Then, on January 25, 1999, J. Peterman declared bankruptcy. A month later, the assets of the company were sold at auction to the midwestern retailer Paul Harris. Because of the *Seinfeld* exposure, the entire bankruptcy was covered on national television. For an entrepreneur, it was the most horrifically public failure imaginable.

Peterman was devastated. Among the traumatic events in his life, from his service in the Marine Corps to seeing his dreams of major league stardom as player in the Pittsburgh Pirates organization disappear with a broken leg in his second season, there is nothing that competes with the bankruptcy. Peterman feels a deep sense of personal responsibility for the company and the people. "J. Peterman was a family company and I was the head of the family. I let my family down," he says soberly when I ask him. It was a reality check for someone who had spent a decade traveling the world and several years in the spotlight as a celebrity. But Peterman, like his brand, is made of sterner stuff. After several weeks of abject depression, he began to pull himself up. It helped when his son-in-law Steve Zahn (who starred with Matthew McConaughey in *Sahara*) and actor Ethan Hawke paid a visit to the ranch. The two pitched in as Peterman laid down the brick floor for the basement of his cabin. The days were full of crushing labor. The evenings gave them time to sip wine and talk. Hawke had good advice for Peterman about the public nature of his downfall, telling him that "Being a celebrity is tricky stuff. People have unrealistic expectations about you. It can distort your whole life."

As he often does, Peterman sought perspective. He did it through literary therapy—expunging his demons by writing a memoir that sold 75,000 copies. The book and speaking engagements also sustained him, as the bankruptcy had left Peterman and Audrey without any income. Speaking to audiences about his experience building J. Peterman also ignited the spark that made him want to try again.

I begin to muse more about Peterman's cabin as we prepare for dinner. While Peterman sautés garlic, I slice tomatoes, onions, and cucumbers for a small tossed salad. In the day that I have spent with Peterman, this is the only time that I've felt fully competent. Peterman has that effect on you. [Show me another CEO who has been on *Oprah* and CNN but still spreads manure and digs postholes.] In addition to having been a Marine and a professional baseball player, Peterman was a private pilot, and even today at normal retirement age he could moonlight as a ranch hand, carpenter, or stone mason. The linguine with sautéed shrimp in a tomato sauce that he throws together offhandedly is excellent. So is the view of the setting sun, which has lingered in the sky until 9 p.m. in this westernmost corner of the Eastern time zone.

We sit on the porch of the cabin, looking over the spread of land rolling away from us. I marvel again at the perfect simplicity of the

Kentucky bluegrass ranch. But it is not a Kentucky experience we are having. We're eating Italian food off of English china with French cutlery, including Laguiole dinner knives from France, sitting on the deck of a cabin built in 1994.

To Peterman, however, this is precisely the point. The world is not what is handed to you, but what you make of it. Peterman's gift is for constructing the world that he wants to live in and crafting it piece by piece from the best of what he finds in other places and other times. His criteria are stringent—the past is only valuable when it is more rugged, functional, and beautiful than modern alternatives. And when it adds factual romance to an everyday item. Peterman has done on a grander scale in his cabin what he accomplishes in the *Owner's Manual:* he creates a beautiful, functional space that feels at once lived in and alive and offers endless opportunity for exploration. You can spend as much time examining the wood grain on a French side table or the assortment of unusual hats hanging next to the Colt on the coat hooks in Peterman's cabin as you can spend imagining how you'll look in the Argentinean polo shirt in the *Owner's Manual:*

---

5 miles west of Buenos Aires you'll find the Hurlingham Polo Club.

Founded by English expats in 1888. Six polo fields, a grand Victorian clubhouse with the Queen's portrait hanging in the main room.

The founders wouldn't recognize the game going on outside.

(continued)

In Argentina, you play the man, not the ball. Riders yell like gauchos and drive their horses into one another at breakneck speed, with violent T-bone collisions. The fearless Argentinians have held the World Polo Championship without interruption since 1949.

This is the shirt they wear to play.

Argentinian Polo Shirt (No. 1634). Robust cotton piqué. Two-button placket. Long sleeves, for play in chilly July and August. The colors and markings are more vivid than in English polo shirts—a matter of machismo, I'd say.

This is the heart of the J. Peterman brand—dissatisfaction with the disposability of modern American society, willingness to construct one's own identity out of borrowings from other times and places, and a purist's eye for quality and detail. This stubborn contrarianism is at the heart of many great brands. Even Nike started its life as a contrarian brand. The "Just Do It" tagline is nothing more than a sneer at the majority of part-time athletes who pretend to work out and find excuses to avoid hitting the road. Nike unabashedly rejected the rest of us in favor of serious athletes. But that attitude attracted us in even greater numbers. Peterman understands, as Nike did, that rejecting consumers to tell people what you stand for is not a bad thing. It is what makes a brand distinctive, what gives it a reason for being. This is the core value that *Seinfeld* nearly destroyed: the massive social imprimatur that *Seinfeld* gave J. Peterman catapulted them into the mainstream.

Through the *Owner's Manual,* Peterman teaches his customers how to turn a coat, a shirt, and a pair of boots into a different attitude toward life. He is the god of small things, weaving empowerment and optimism into the threads of his wares. Subscribing to the J. Peterman philosophy means taking control of your life and your world and rejecting the notion that the world is just what it is. Peterman's world is whatever he makes of it. And, much like Monticello was for Thomas Jefferson, the making is a lifetime pursuit.

As with other successful entrepreneurs who have accidentally built large brands, like Roxanne Quimby of Burt's Bees, Jake Burton of Burton Snowboards, or "Ma" Barker of Columbia Sportswear, the essence of Peterman's brand is not in a marketing plan or a "brand book" but in its creator's DNA. Peterman did not set out to craft the J. Peterman brand in a particular way—he just did what he thought was right. And the typical behaviors I have come to expect from these entrepreneurs are all manifest in Peterman.

Peterman has built a core of fanatically devoted employees and consumers who have a real stake in his success. He doesn't agree with the way other folks do things and doesn't hesitate to let people know what he thinks. In the end, this makes him an original. It is this authenticity that makes the J. Peterman brand unique and valuable.

Peterman says that one of the attractions of the ranch, for him, is the lack of sounds, the splendid isolation. I presume by this that he means man-made sounds, because the night air is alive with a cacophony of insects as I pad into the guest bedroom in Peterman's cabin. But there is something comforting about the 200-year-old reclaimed oak floor against my bare feet, and about the solid spruce beams staring down at me as I lie on one of the two single beds, and soon I am awakened by morning light from the window. Peterman is already up when I appear downstairs and he continues to philos- ophize as we take a last stroll around the cabin after breakfast. There is sadness in him, the residual pain of an entrepreneur who has been stopped just short of his dreams and forced to restart. J. Peterman 2.0 is a smarter, saner operation than the one he piloted the first time around. Two years after the bankruptcy auction, Paul Harris Ltd., the British retailer who had bought rights to the J. Peterman name, went bankrupt in the United States. Peterman gathered some close friends as investors and purchased the name back from Schottenstein Bernstein, the bankruptcy liquidators. Then he quietly restarted the J. Peterman Company in Lexington. Seventy-five percent of his employees are people who returned from the original company.

The new J. Peterman is growing by 20 percent a year and is adequately capitalized, unlike the original business that doubled each year and operated on a razor-thin cashflows. Peterman no longer has to wonder each season how he will finance the merchandise for the next *Owner's Manual.* Inventory is more tightly controlled, and the core team of merchants walks in lockstep with Peterman's eccentric vision. Indeed, Peterman is still not afraid to make the odd gesture to let his customers know that he has not lost his quirky appeal. I'm in the midst of interviewing his chief women's merchant, Paula Collins, when Peterman drags in a huge crate that he cracks open with a crowbar. It contains a periscope manufactured in East Germany for use on the Berlin Wall. Just why someone would buy such an odd item is not clear to Collins or Peterman, but they marvel at the solid craftsmanship and agree to pick up a few for the *Owner's Manual.*

Ironically, one of the investors in the new J. Peterman is the actor John O'Hurley. Peterman had met O'Hurley on the *Fox after Breakfast* morning show several years earlier when the show did a segment on "introducing the two Petermans." When I ask John O'Hurley about this meeting, he smiles and says, "We literally didn't meet each other until we were on camera. I thought that he was rather quiet. He was uncomfortable with the celebrity and the personal attachment to the brand." But when the two started to talk, they found that they had much in common. "I live the same life as Peterman," O'Hurley tells me as we lounge in his suite at the Trump International Hotel and Tower on Columbus Circle in Manhattan. In fact, O'Hurley has just arrived from South Africa and will be heading to Spain in a matter of days. "He would send me clothes and I would send him wine," O'Hurley says of the early days of his friendship with Peterman. I ask him about the differences between them and O'Hurley smiles. "Peterman is frugal," he says. "We always have great arguments over the cost of a great bottle of wine. Peterman doesn't believe that things that are great should be priced out of reach." On the subject of the J. Peterman brand, however, the two agree—and O'Hurley speaks surprisingly like a marketer. "J. Peterman answers a need for authenticity in a world that is losing authenticity at a catastrophic rate," he says. "Authenticity is an endangered species and that makes Peterman a citizen of the world."

Peterman does wonder, however, if he'll have the energy to complete the turnaround he has begun. He is a generation older than he was when he first started J. Peterman and looks forward to spending more time on the ranch and traveling the world for his own pleasure. He has the impatience of all great entrepreneurs combined with the world-weariness of someone who has seen it all before. But just as quickly as he sinks into the mood, he picks himself up and soon we are bouncing along the access road to his cabin in his pickup truck. As we stop at the gate to the ranch, he takes pains to show me how to lock the chain-link around the posts behind us. "You never know when you might be back," he says and smiles.

THE CONTRARIAN: CRAIG NEWMARK (CRAIGSLIST)

Boyfriend with A/C needed - w4m

Date: 2006-07-31, 6:40PM EDT

I am looking for a moderately attractive man between the ages of 18 and 40 who has air conditioning in his bedroom. As the temperature is slated to reach in the 100s this week, my need for a boyfriend with air conditioning is especially pertinent.

This arrangement is intended for the month of August, however, an Indian summer may extend our relationship.

P.S. No fatties.

I'm standing in front of the University of California–San Francisco Medical Center with Craig Newmark, the founder of the online classified site craigslist. Craig, who bears a passing resemblance to the actor Jason Alexander, is talking to his doctor about having his gallbladder removed. Although Newmark is having the surgery for the usual reason (gallstones), he has also been enrolled into a clinical trial. Craig apparently has a unique constitution that allows him to tolerate the vitamin niacin, and he's been taking supplements. The study is to determine how niacin causes low levels of cholesterol to be expressed by the liver, and the medical team will take a biopsy from Craig when the doctor removes his gall bladder. Craig has come to UCSF on this sunny spring morning for his final presurgical visit. And brought me. I spend the better part of an hour watching stick figures run around a track from what might be the best view of any doctors' waiting room in the country. Then Craig emerges and we leave the office. Almost immediately, we run into Craig's doctor in the elevator. We walk outside, Craig introduces me, and the doctor takes the opportunity to explain his research work to us. The doctor tries to clarify the point of his research, and Craig seems to understand him, but he is speaking in technical language; like Charlie Brown in the *Peanuts* cartoons, all I hear is "Wah-wah-wah-wah-wah." As our paths diverge, Craig thanks the doctor and puts his hand out to shake. The doctor fumbles with his clipboard, and I suddenly realize he has a handful of test tubes in his right hand that are preventing him from shaking Craig's hand. The test tubes are full of blood. Craig's blood. It's not the way I expected the morning to go.

On the other hand, I am a world ahead of where I started out with Craig. Flash back two hours earlier: I arrive on his doorstep at 8:30 A.M. to be greeted with a gruff, "Who's there?" When I identify myself, Craig does not seem to recognize me. After I hand him a copy of our e-mail correspondence, he tells me that we have canceled this meeting. I realize that he may be correct. A few days earlier he had informed me he would be in New York in two weeks' time and asked if

I would like to meet in Greenwich Village. I agreed, thinking that this would be in addition to our meeting at his house in San Francisco. Craig reasonably assumed that we would cancel our meeting at his place. So he isn't quite dressed when I catch him at home. He asks me to wait across the street and says he'll call my cell phone when he is ready. Twenty minutes later he does just that. Then he lets me know that he has an errand to run after getting coffee, but that I can accompany him. That errand is the doctor's visit.

It's an apt meeting with Craig Newmark, who has maintained a mysterious and reclusive air even as he makes regular public appearances. If you haven't heard of craigslist, then chances are you're either over 40 or not living in one of 450 cities in the United States or 52 other countries for which craigslist has classifieds. For the rest of us, craigslist has replaced the yellow pages, the newspaper classifieds, and Internet dating sites as the best place to find something—or someone. Virtually anything you can imagine is getting bought and sold on craigslist at a given moment. A random search of the New York site on a summer afternoon turns up posts hawking bikes, boats, cars, a 7.5-foot-tall fake Christmas tree ($30, in Williamsburg), a dry-chemical fire extinguisher (if the tree doesn't work out as expected), a ferret cage, and mounted deer heads.

The design of craigslist is extremely simple. It has no graphics and no ads. The craigslist Web site is text based and has multiple categories, which include Community (everything from activities and events to rideshare and pet groups), Jobs, Services, For Sale, Housing, Gigs (freelance opportunities), Discussion Forums (everything here from vegan to etiquette), and Personals. Posting on craigslist or answering an ad is simple and, with two exceptions, it's also free. The two exceptions are jobs (prospective employers pay $75 per listing in San Francisco and $25 in New York City, Los Angeles, Washington,

D.C., Boston, Seattle, and San Diego) and housing ($10 per listing in New York). "Free" is a powerful concept. and for craigslist the free listings have created a huge community with over twenty-two million users and an astounding eight billion page views a month. The modestly named www.craigslist.org is the seventh-largest Web site on the planet.

not overly managed

To understand what craigslist *is*, you first have to understand a long list of *not*s. The service is not a public company, but it's also not a charity. Craig Newmark does not run it. A major corporation does not own craigslist, but neither is the company entirely free from corporate influence. (eBay purchased 25 percent of the equity of craigslist from a former shareholder in 2004 and has a seat on the craigslist board of directors.) Posts on craigslist are not edited the way a newspaper is or moderated the way a discussion board might be.

All of these *not*'s have helped craigslist become what it actually is—a powerful expression of the local community in each city where it operates. Instead of relying on staff to police the classified listings, craigslist makes it easy to "flag" offensive posts by clicking in the upper right hand corner of the listing. The flags that can be applied to a listing are "Miscategorized," "Prohibited," "Spam," "Discussion," and "Best of." The second and third flags are the serious ones, and if a post accumulates a certain number of them (which can vary from category to category, city to city and day to day) it is automatically removed from the site. On the discussion forums, the craigslist staff reviews flagged items. This is Craig's full-time job—he calls it customer service.

As we sit down for coffee near the medical center, I ask Craig how he deals with people who use craigslist for scams or to harass others. "For fraud issues, we work with law enforcement," he says carefully. "For the rest, I try to use reason. This works with most people." Craig is uniquely effective at policing the community he fathered. Even after harassing several women, posting hate speech, or improperly representing oneself as, say, single, most people will prove surprisingly cooperative when they get an e-mail from Craig himself asking them to desist.

Craig's life can be drawn in a relatively straight line between the neighborhoods of Cole Valley, where his two-story bungalow sits, and Inner Sunset, where a converted Victorian house serves as the home for the 23 people who work full time to keep craigslist running. The distance between the two points is about a mile, although (this being San Francisco) the vertical distance is as relevant as the horizontal, and not inconsiderable. From the UCSF campus, we walk down the hill into the Inner Sunset neighborhood, where with a single turn we arrive at the two-story Victorian that houses craigslist.

There are 11 main rooms in the craigslist headquarters—including an office that Craig shares with CEO Jim Buckmaster. There is also a bathroom and a small kitchen, but it is a very modest space. The office seems like it would be a tranquil place to work. I cannot say this with certainty, because it is clear that the craigslist DNA has created a tightly knit group. Nobody smiles or says hello to me as Newmark shows me around. Even the CEO barely acknowledges Craig's introduction before turning back to his work. There's an aggressive anticorporate scent in the air of the old Victorian (Craig calls it "intensity of purpose"), which seems unnaturally quiet during my visit.

Craig's desk is a large wooden surface dominated by a huge computer screen. He sits back to back with Buckmaster, and this arrangement makes them look more like college roommates working on separate term papers than colleagues. Craig has a bookshelf above his desk with some current reading, including Anthony Everitt's biography of the Roman Emperor Augustus and Glenn Reynolds' *An*

Army of Davids. Then there are photos—including a picture of Craig with Stephen Colbert, and on his deck one of birds——and finally a *Simpsons* diorama.

Shortly after we arrive, Craig plows into his work. Watching Craig on the computer is a little like watching a chef dice onions, or a craftsman in Colonial Williamsburg spin cotton on a gin. Craig moves so quickly and efficiently through e-mail that I find it difficult to follow what he's actually doing. The screen flashes as he moves seamlessly from window to window. I try to ask him a few questions, but it becomes apparent that I'm disturbing Buckmaster, so we agree that on my next visit to San Francisco, I will observe Craig working from home where he can talk. Nobody looks up as I slip out of the office.

---

air guitar

Date: 2007-09-11, 5:09PM PDT

Left-handed vintage air guitar for free. All that's needed is new strings and a good dusting.

Two weeks later, I'm walking through the western part of Greenwich Village to meet Craig for an early dinner. He is in town for a conference and to speak at an NYU class. Craig loves Greenwich Village, so I pick a nice café/restaurant. He is already seated when I arrive.

I ask Craig about the Missed Connections section of the personal classifieds on craigslist. This is one of the most popular features on craigslist and may constitute one of craigslist's supreme contributions to Western society—namely, a second chance. Missed Connections are real-world encounters where one person or the other regrets not having taken the next step. These classifieds literally give love a second chance, as the foiled romantic can post a note on craigslist and hope that hot guy or girl in question will see it and respond. Buckmaster came up with the idea for this category in September 2000 after reading a number of personals he characterizes as "You-smiled-at-me-on-the-subway-but-I-was-too-shy-to-say-anything-would-you-like-to-go-out-for-coffee." Craig, slipping into what Nick Denton, founder of the celebrity-obsessed blog Gawker, has called Craig's "Chauncey Gardiner" mode, says only, "Sometimes you meet someone, there's chemistry, but you never get to exchange numbers." Just like Peter Sellers' character in *Being There*, Newmark has a way of stating the perfectly obvious with no apparent irony and making you feel like you've gained a new insight. He is not egoless, but he is far closer to it than the average midlevel corporate manager.

Craig started craigslist in early 1995. He was working for the investment company Charles Schwab at the time as a systems architect. His formal job was to help with network security. Informally, Craig became an Internet evangelist in the early days of the Internet. This was a time when most people had no idea how the Internet could be used. In the beginning, craigslist was not a Web site at all but a simple e-mail list. Craig would mail his friends a list of local technology- and arts-related events. The list grew over time and eventually exceeded the capacity of Craig's e-mail program. At that point, Newmark realized that it would be simple to classify the events and put them into folders on a list server. This required a name. Although Craig wanted to call his list "sf-events," several friends, including another Web designer named Anthony Batt, urged him to call it craigslist. Craig designed the Web site to save himself time by allowing his friends to post their own events. Over the course of the first couple of years, people started requesting new categories. Early additions were jobs, items for sale, and apartments. The site benefited both from the upsurge of interest in the Internet in the late 1990s and from the explosion of the housing market in San Francisco. For the thousands of Internet workers migrating to San Francisco in that era, having a quick, cheap, easily accessed site to view and respond to apartment listings was invaluable. By 1997, craigslist had grown to over a million page views per month and was fast becoming part of everyday life in the San Francisco Bay area. Want an apartment? craigslist. A new job? craigslist. Sell old furniture? craigslist.

The content and page views kept expanding rapidly, and with them came requests to expand craigslist to new geographical areas. As this volume exploded, the administrative burden of maintaining the site and dealing with problems was beginning to overwhelm Craig. So was the cost of the storage and bandwidth for craigslist. Craig had been funding the site from his pocket, but it was fast becoming too expensive and too time-consuming to continue as a part-time operation.

Craig's first response, in 1998, was to turn to the craigslist community for help. A number of volunteers approached Craig, offering to help him run the site. "It wasn't a bad idea, but as it turns out people weren't all that reliable and the results for the site weren't good." He also created an income stream for craigslist by charging for job postings, which was the first user charge for any craigslist service. Finally, in 1999, Craig left his day job and incorporated the company. He also started hiring people to help him. Initially, they worked out of his house. "My place was able to support an office of six or so comfortably," Craig says, referring to his previous apartment, also in the Cole Valley. "When it got to be eight—not so comfortable."

In 2000, Craig made several significant changes to craigslist. First, Craig gave away equity to his employees (neither Craig nor

Buckmaster will comment on the numbers, but a single employee ended up with 25 percent of the company.) Secondly, Craig demoted himself and made Jim Buckmaster (whom he had recently hired as lead programmer) the CEO. I ask Craig why he stepped down as CEO of craigslist. He smiles wryly as he answers, "I was beginning to realize that I'm not a very good manager, and some people were kind enough to point that out to me. I also remembered that back at IBM I read a paper that suggested that people who are good at starting companies are not good at keeping them going." That year, craigslist also moved into office space. It was a real business.

After Newmark turned management over to Jim Buckmaster, craigslist embarked on a blistering growth program, expanding to eight cities in the first year alone. The decision to put Buckmaster in charge seems to have paid off for both craigslist, which has grown exponentially while adding few costs, and for Craig, who can live a saner life than he might be able to if he were still responsible for managing day-to-day operations. Buckmaster also added personals to craigslist in 2000, and it was personals that really put the site on the cultural map. Like some weird kind of catalyst, personals were the element in the recipe for craigslist that caused it to bubble over. Before personals, craigslist was very useful. After personals, craigslist rapidly became an icon in cities all around the United States.

Craig's decision to give equity to employees did not work out as well. "I gave out equity thinking that we're a community service, but I could still be tempted to sell, so if I give some equity that's less likely to happen. It backfired on me—I've never been really tempted to sell, whereas [one of the employees] sold his equity." The sale in 2004 put craigslist in bed with a huge corporate partner—eBay. At the time, Craig and Jim Buckmaster were publicly supportive of the sale because they believed that eBay could help craigslist with security issues. That outward stance still holds, but you have to wonder how Newmark and Buckmaster feel now that eBay has started competing with craigslist in the United States. eBay is challenging craigslist with a free classified service called Kijiji that they've operated for several years outside the country.

We're just between the lunch and dinner hours at the café in Greenwich Village. I order a small salad while Craig contemplates whether the soup of the day is too cheesy for him. Then I ask Craig about his work schedule. His days go something like this:

8 A.M. – Wake up

8–10 A.M. – Work at home

10–10:30 A.M. – Shower

10:30–11:30 A.M. – Coffee at Reverie

11:30 A.M.–12:30 P.M. – Walk to the office, stop for lunch along the way

12:30–5 P.M. – Work at the office

5:30–7 P.M. – Work from home

7–9 P.M. – Dinner, relax

9–11 P.M. – Work from home

11 P.M. – *The Daily Show, The Colbert Report*

When I ask Craig what he does on weekends, he says that he will sometimes see friends, his girlfriend Eileen, or family, but that usually he works on both Saturday and Sunday. Then I ask him about his last vacation. He scratches his beard for a moment, thoughtfully. "I really can't remember. It must have been more than 10 years ago." When I press him, he says simply, "I'm not very good at vacation. I did go to Hawaii a couple of years ago, but the ticket was paid for and I was working and using the business center at the hotel extensively." Craig recently went to Israel, but this too combined a speaking schedule and a good deal of work with some light tourism.

Then I ask Craig about his personal goals. I'm surprised to hear that they have nothing to do with craigslist: "I'd like to save the world, but I'm not smart enough. If I can get other people to do it, that would be better. We need better journalism and better investigative reporting—that's why I have been funding some of these things." He funds the Center for Citizen Media and a program at NYU and is on the board of the Sunlight Foundation, which focuses on bringing unsavory activities in Washington to light. Our dinner is on the day of the Virginia Tech massacre, and Craig is particularly upset that people are using the tragedy as a platform to push their agenda on gun control, whether from a pro (armed students would have stopped the rampage sooner) or anti (a clinically depressed person should not have a gun) position.

I hit a wall when I ask Craig about his material goals, because he doesn't seem to have any. He points out that he had a comfortable life as a systems architect before he started craigslist and that he has bought a house that he likes in a nice neighborhood. He has a nice TV and several computers. He strains to think of what else he might desire. "Money is a consideration; we need it to live in our society. But once you make enough, what's the point of making more? I mean, at some point I might go middle age crazy, grow a comb-forward and put my name on buildings . . . but right now I drive an old Prius."

In both of our meetings, Craig has described himself as "lazy," and I ask him about that. I've calculated that he works somewhere between 60 and 80 hours in an average week, so I am having trouble understanding why he would consider himself slothful. "There are people who are much more proactive than me and who actually do something when things upset them." Craig points to two bloggers, libertarian Glenn Reynolds of Instapundit and liberal Markos Moulitsas of Daily Kos, as exemplars who have the drive to change things they care about. The reality, as I reflect on it, is simply that Craig has exactly the life that he wants. Work is his amusement, his pastime, and the only guilt he feels comes from the fact that he could be doing more to pursue his serious goals.

Over the course of the meal, we've been handed off from our original waiter to two waitresses. The second waitress, a 21-year-old attractive brunette, is a trainee named Mia, and the senior waitress introduces her and explains the training. Craig asks Mia coyly, "How do they advertise for jobs around here?" She answers with the name of his Web site. "What do you think of that?" he asks. "Cool," she says, "Really useful." Then there is a pause. It seems like a moment where Craig would like to be recognized, but he's too modest to reveal himself, so I do. "This is Craig from craigslist," I tell Mia. The two waitresses do a double take and begin chattering excitedly at the same time. "Cool! I got my apartment from you. Great idea!" says the senior waitress. Mia adds, "You make my whole life work. I got my first apartment, this job, last job, my first sublet, and my boyfriend from craigslist!"

As they walk away, I tell Craig that adulation is a nice job perk. "I'm still surprised—and pleased—when people say that," he says. He does seem a little bemused by the success of craigslist, and he is one of the very few entrepreneurs that I have met who acknowledges that luck and chance were factors in his success. Craig was not the only person sending around lists of events to his friends in the '90s. He wasn't the only one that turned these lists into a business. An Argentinean named Bernardo Joselevich built a good-sized event list in New York during the dotcom boom and still makes his living from the list *customizable*

by charging for event listings and solo e-mail campaigns. Although Bernardo never translated his event list into a broader social exchange, several others did. But no other service captured the imagination of the public quite like craigslist.

What makes craigslist great? It is convenient and easy to use, that's true. But the bigger element may be that it has taken the most moribund section of the newspaper—classified listings—and injected it with life. When I ask Craig how he managed this, he again defers responsibility. "I agree with the result, but the people who did it are the people who use the site. Our role in making it happen is just to get out of the way. Some sites try to dictate to people how their site should be used. Our take on that is that people should choose how they want the site to be used." When I ask Craig to give me an example, he points to the use of craigslist after Hurricane Katrina. "In New Orleans, survivors began to use it as a network to locate each other and as a way to coordinate jobs and housing. People feel connected by all of this. I've given up on a doctrinaire definition of community, but if people feel connected to other people, that's a community."

Taken this way, craigslist mirrors some very advanced thinking about brands, including work being done by Alex Wipperfürth, who wrote *Brand Hijack*. Wipperfurth has systematically studied brands like Dr. Martens, In-N-Out Burger, and Pabst Blue Ribbon to see how consumers have taken control of brands and made them their own. These consumers use the brands in unexpected ways and customize them in a way that transforms them. "Brand hijacks" create brands that are more meaningful to these consumers and that gain currency with a broader audience. Craig's site *craigslist* was a hijacked brand from the beginning. Craig calls the brand a "public service," and it is clear that a number of his bigger decisions—including the fateful decision to give away over 50 percent of the company to employees—stem from that mission. The brand never ceased to become relevant to its core audience because it has been the users themselves who drive change on the site. In spite of the liberal politics of its employees, the site is fundamentally conservative in nature. It evolves only after the need for change becomes critical. Thus, both new features and new geographies only come on line after a significant base of support already exists for them.

One criticism of craigslist is that it is a jungle. Whom you meet and what you get on craigslist are both pretty random and might not be any better than what you would encounter on the streets of a big city. Unlike eBay, there is no reputation management system where users can rate transactions and sellers. The personals also carry risk. With no cost to post or respond to personals, there are some truly strange people on craigslist. A craigslist meeting always has both the danger and the thrill of the inherent risk of the unknown. When Craig accepted his Person of the Year honor at the ninth annual Webby Awards in 2005 (with a five-word acceptance speech), Rob Corddry, the comic correspondent from *The Daily Show*, waved him off with the memorable line, "Congratulations, Craig. Thanks for helping me get chlamydia."

r downfall (don't have it)

I ask Craig about the idea of adding reputation management to craigslist and he says, "I think the time has come—actually that it's overdue—but I've been wrong a bunch of times. Part of all of this is that we need better means of authenticating people." What's interesting here is that I don't get the sense he's just talking about internal resistance from the craigslist staff—he means that, in some way, technology is not advanced enough to make quality control a straightforward task, and that the community may not be ready for quality control. Craig is unique in having made a personal mission out of, as he puts it, "not messing up things that work."

Celeb Talk Show is looking for FRIENDS THAT ARE CON-STANTLY COMPETING

Date: 2007-07-19, 1:10PM EDT

Do you have a friend that you are always competing with? Do you have a rival that always tries to one up you? Here is your opportunity to find out who the better woman is once and for all. We are looking for women who want to appear on a celebrity hosted talk show with their rival friend to put their skills to the test.

Please respond with a picture of you and your friend and a brief summary of the competitive relationship.

I am back in San Francisco, standing outside of Craig's door. I knock hesitantly, wondering if I have again miscommunicated. This time, though, Craig is expecting me and he is fully dressed. I get a brief tour of his Cole Valley bungalow, which is larger than it appears from outside. Craig lives on a street that makes a U-shaped diversion up the hill from one of the main roads in the Cole Valley. It is an expensive neighborhood filled mostly with small structures tucked up one against another like crows on a telephone wire straining to see the sunset. His house is tastefully furnished with modern but comfortable furniture. A large plasma TV commands the living room. "I like *The Daily Show, Colbert, The Simpsons, Letterman,* and anything with good storytelling," he says. Behind this is a well-appointed kitchen and, beside that, his office. Although I've entered on the ground level, the bungalow is built into the side of the hill and there is a bedroom downstairs. A simple stained hardwood desk dominates Craig's office with a 24-inch monitor and Zonbox PC running Linux. The office looks out onto a deck, from which he has a commanding view of the Twin Peaks area of San Francisco.

As we step out onto the deck, Craig shows me his bird feeder and the Web cam that points at it. Web cams are cameras that continuously stream video onto a Web site. They have practical uses (one of the Westin properties in Hawaii sports a Web cam that locals check obsessively to see the surfing conditions), illicit uses (so-called "voyeur" cameras for sex or nanny cams that allow nervous parents to check on the treatment of their toddlers), and civic uses (recreating C-SPAN for your local town council). Still, pointing a Web cam at a bird feeder sitting inside the city limits of one of the largest cities in the United States seems like an odd choice to me. But Craig assures me that the Web cam has a following, and who could doubt him?

Craig spends at least half of his working time in his home office, so I am curious to see how he works. Since we're alone, I am able to ask him what he's doing, which is the only way I'll be able to tell, as he seems to move even faster on his home computer than the one at work. As he starts massaging the keyboard, Craig's online personality emerges—one part beat cop, one-part therapist. The first problem for the day is a man who's been ranting and harassing people on the discussion boards. Craig knows the poster from previous incidents, but he's sympathetic. "He's off his meds." He temporarily blocks the man's access to craigslist and sends him an e-mail.

The next case is someone who is using the discussion boards to advertise. "That's a big no-no and he's been warned." This guy has his ads pulled, his posting privileges suspended, and his i.p. address blocked. Next Craig is called to mediate some vicious bickering and harassment on the pet discussion boards. This involves the question of whether it is legal or acceptable to breed and sell animals out of one's backyard. (Presumably this is a problem if one lives in the city.)

Then Craig tackles an unlicensed roommate service in New York City that is trying to get around legal requirements by using craigslist. He gets in touch with the NYC Department of Consumer Affairs to alert them. Also, in the New York City real estate section, a broker has been posting in the owner's section, another big no-no. This person is using a professional spammer to post the ads, so Craig looks at the i.p. address, finds all of the posts tying to that address, and pulls them. There are 132 ads. Craig makes a note to himself to contact the broker's Internet service provider.

A frequent problem on craigslist is people who post offensive or controversial topics (often racist or otherwise bigoted) with the intention of picking fights. "We call these people 'trolls,'" he says. "They're trying to get attention." Craig reads a flagged post, an angry rant about women, and he sighs audibly, something he does very often. This particular troll strikes Craig as more needy and sad than dangerous, and he lets the post go. Next he reads e-mail from a craigslist user who has been scammed while buying a car. The site gives no guarantees to buyers and sellers, but Craig is genuinely upset when people are cheated. Craig tells the victim to contact the FBI and offers his help in locating the offender.

values craig has are reflected in how site is run

I begin to see the appeal of the work that Craig has chosen for himself. He keeps a finger on the pulse of the community he spawned and also actively defends it from trespassers. Even if he does not run craigslist, Craig spends his days transmitting the value structure he created. Getting a warning directly from Craig is not something most people are likely to forget.

All at once, Craig stands up and tells me it's time for coffee. It is his favorite time of day—time to go to Reverie.

By his own account, Craig Newmark had a fairly normal childhood in suburban New Jersey, at least until the age of 13 when his father died of lung cancer. Craig was a prototypical nerd, wearing a pocket protector and thick glasses in high school. When I gamely tell him that I wore a Texas Instruments programmable calculator on my belt for one regrettable year in junior high school, he smiles and tells me that I must be at least a dozen years younger than him (exactly true) because his generation used slide rules. Craig left home to attend Case Western Reserve in Cleveland, getting two degrees in computer sciences. Then he went to work for IBM in Boca Raton as a systems programmer. After 6 years in Boca Raton, he was persuaded to move to Detroit. "There was a woman involved—that lasted only about two weeks. But I did spend 10 years in Detroit." He stayed with IBM through this period and for a year in Pittsburgh, at which time IBM began laying people off and he decided to leave. Newmark got a job with Charles Schwab and moved to San Francisco, where he has remained ever since.

Your pack of cigarettes for my brand new monitor, printer cables—$10
Date: 2007-07-19, 4:20PM EDT

I really need a pack of cigarettes, but I'm low on cash. I'm willing to trade.

1. Brand New Black Dell CRT 14″ Color monitor
2. Brand New Unopened pack of computer cables.

Heck, you can even buy a pack, and call me . . . $10, if I have to bring everything to you. Fare [sic] trade, if you can meet me.

Call me now.

Reverie is a nice local coffeehouse in Cole Valley that might be mistaken for a low-key Starbucks if not for the pleasant garden seating out back. I ask Craig about the stereotype of craigslist as a virtual marketplace. "It's been described," he says, "accurately, I think, as a flea market—a market in the ancient sense." And it is true that craigslist seems to have recreated the rough-and-tumble feeling of the Grand Bazaar in Istanbul or the Chatuchak weekend market in Bangkok. What fascinates me even more is why this has happened. It's not just because people can sell anything that they want and write their own ad copy. That is true on eBay as well. But eBay looks and feels like a commercial site, whereas the postings on craigslist are infused with the personality of the seller. This is not just true of the personals on craigslist—even the description of a desk or a plea to exchange Yankees tickets for Mets can reveal the soul of the writer. Craig understands this and, more than anything, it is the sense that he has created a real community that gives him satisfaction.

While we're at Reverie, I ask Craig about his girlfriend, Eileen. Craig has been single his entire life. The two of them have now been dating for three years. When I ask him about wedding plans, Craig says cryptically, "I'm not particularly interested in ceremonies." Then he hastens to add that he is talking literally about just the ceremony—not the idea of being married. Craig met Eileen at Reverie and says that he approached her—which is somewhat difficult for me to imagine. When I speak to her later, though, Eileen confirms this. "I was coming off a relationship where I was dating this dashing, crazy, unreliable, bad person. I wanted to connect to someone who was a little more real. I actually went to Reverie to try to make friends in the neighborhood. When I met Craig it was the second time I had been in there. When I walked in, I was on my way to a dance class and kind of in a hurry. Craig was sitting against a wall and he was looking at me. Really looking, staring. I thought there was something wrong and asked, 'Is this seat taken?' He said, 'No, it's just that you're so beautiful.' The guy sitting at the table next to Craig rolled his eyes. He obviously thought Craig was being ridiculous. But I liked the fact that Craig said something so genuine. I actually talked to Craig to spite that other guy. In California, guys have a tendency to be so cool—it's so annoying." I ask Eileen her initial impression of Craig and she laughs. "He was this nice, honest, traditional guy. Exactly the opposite of my last relationship."

The big question in my mind is whether Eileen knew who Craig was before she decided to date him. She immediately admits that she did. "We had that 'what do you do' exchange and he said he had a community Web site. But I knew his name was Craig, so I asked him if he was Craig of craigslist and he said yes. He had already asked me out and I was being coy, but at that point I decided to go out with him because I thought that it would at least be a great story to tell—going out on a date with Craig of craigslist." But when she actually went out with Craig, he charmed her (and, indeed, it is hard not to be charmed by Craig's guileless honesty), so she went out with him again. Eventually, it became a relationship. When I ask her about any challenges with Craig, she mentions vacations. "That's something we have to work on. I don't want to go my whole life without taking a vacation. I'll have to organize it. He doesn't want to go anyplace without a wi-fi connection. You know how it is with guys, it's always something."

Do nice guys exist?
Date: 2003-06-18, 9:11PM EDT

25 years old, Chinese-American, Female, 5′2″-ish, Graduate student, painter seeks a . . . nice guy. Does he exist?

Aw so cute

> I am a friendly, easy-going, and open-minded girl.
>
> I like the simple things (nature, a good night's sleep, etc.)
>
> I like being silly (i'm a fan of old Bugs Bunny cartoons & Monty Python)
>
> I love music (have eclectic tastes, my Favorites include Radiohead, Aimee Mann, & The Smiths, but I also enjoy Debussy, Buena Vista club, and Chinese pop). I like art (from Calvin & Hobbes strips to juicy Lucien Freud paintings).
>
> If you like these same kinds of things, please email me back so we can chat or perhaps meet.
>
> **(Please don't respond if you're a big jerk)

In the middle of my series of conversations with Craig, I attend a craigslist wedding. I don't actually realize that it's a craigslist wedding until I'm about to walk into the ceremony and I see a set of e-mails displayed on a bulletin board. The first e-mail starts with "Saw your ad on craigslist." The couple has lost the original craigslist posting that set off the exchange, but Craig is able to help me rescue it (above).

The couple is a perfect embodiment of the craigslist ethos. They come from very different communities, which leads to the interesting juxtaposition of a Quaker ceremony (held in a New Jersey meeting house that first opened for business before the Revolutionary War) followed by a traditional Chinese reception with an eight-course meal. On the surface, the bride and groom look like they might have nothing in common, yet they're remarkably similar in tastes and temperament. Both are teachers and musicians, reserved and polite. The wedding favor is a CD of them singing duets together. This kind of pairing might be routine in large cities these days, where a mishmash of social groups rub elbows and interconnect through shared interests. But for singles not lucky enough to have the right person right at hand, craigslist has proved to be a powerful social lubricant, oiling the cogs of the dating game.

As Craig finishes his coffee at Reverie and my watch tells me it's time to say my goodbyes and head for the airport, I'm still prodding him to see if he has any larger material aspirations in his life. After all, this is a guy who founded a company that some analysts have estimated as having earned $55 million last year alone with only 23 employees and relatively low operating costs. This guy ought to be living on a yacht and bathing in champagne. "Come on, Craig," I say. "What do you really want in life—what personal desires or goals do you have that haven't been met?" He smiles and shakes his head. "None really, although I would like my OQO handheld computer to be delivered . . ." and he begins explaining the coolness of Linux handheld computers to me. So I ask him when he thinks he'll retire. "My exit strategy is death," Craig says. I believe him.

4 really committed

THE TINKERER:
GARY ERICKSON
(CLIF BAR)

The trip from San Francisco to the small office of the Clif Bar Family Winery & Farm in St. Helena takes about an hour and a half but spans different worlds. You can either drive over the Golden Gate Bridge, which leaps northwards off the isthmus that holds San Francisco, and continue through Sausalito, Petaluma, and Santa Rosa, then turn eastwards in Fulton and finally backtrack south to reach St. Helena, or you can head due east over the Bay Bridge to Oakland, then turn north and drive through Vallejo and Napa. I choose the latter route, and the chirpy female British voice on my GPS unit guides me through the confusing maze of San Francisco streets to the Bay Bridge. It is not actually one bridge. In fact, two complete suspension bridges connect San Francisco to Yerba Buena Island, which sits in the middle of San Francisco Bay. At that point, the old-world charms of San Francisco are forgotten and you're facing the modern city and industrial port of Oakland. The bridge continues from Yerba Buena, as a double-tower cantilever span is joined to five truss bridges and a truss causeway, which makes landfall in Oakland. This architectural hodgepodge is not as appealing to my eyes as the vermillion rust of its six-month-younger—and far more famous—sibling to the north, but it is the more commercially vital link for San Francisco.

The transition upon leaving the city of San Francisco is striking. The Oakland naval supply center sits just south of the bridge, so the view to the right as you cross into Oakland is of looming metal dinosaur skeletons, which are actually cargo cranes poised to recover containers from ships. As odd as this sight is, I am looking past the port. I strain my eyes to see all the way past Fremont and Milpitas to Mount Hamilton, some 40 miles distant on the far side of San Jose. It was on this peak, in November 1990, that Clif Bar was born.

On that day, two cyclists were struggling up Mount Hamilton late in the afternoon as the sun began to recede over the horizon. Jay Thomas had lured his friend Gary Erickson—with whom he'd trekked across Europe—out on the ride. The plan was to cover 125 miles that day. That was a healthy distance for the two competition-level cyclists. Jay had plotted a new route, however, and the pair passed the 120-mile point on top of Mount Hamilton and realized that 60 miles of hard riding stood between them and the end of their journey. Erickson had packed six PowerBars that day and he had already eaten five. He needed to finish the last bar, but as he started chewing his stomach turned and he couldn't swallow his first bite.

Elite cyclists use their body's entire reserve of energy to complete long-distance rides. Food is literally fuel for them, just as it is for an automobile. About four years earlier, a marathon runner named Brian Maxwell had created the PowerBar. Maxwell's idea was to take the bulk and complexity out of eating on the go for long-distance athletes by packaging up the nutrients and calories necessary to resupply energy in a convenient form. Although the bar was not really necessary for runners, who could carbo-load before racing, it was an instant success with bikers, who routinely had to carry bulky food with them on rides. The PowerBar was an elegant solution to a long-standing problem for bikers, but it did not taste like food. Maxwell's paradigm for the PowerBar was fuel, and the PowerBar had a chewy, artificial texture that did not entirely resemble anything in nature. Cyclists called it the "<u>bitter pill</u>," but they loved the fact that it kept them pedaling.

Gary Erickson grew up baking pastries and other sweets with his Greek grandmother, Kali. He was born into a family that loved food, and that love was in him. When he realized that he just couldn't eat another PowerBar, it dawned on him that this was a problem that he could solve. Erickson suddenly imagined a bar that supplied the same nutrients and calories as the PowerBar in the same compact form but tasted like a cookie instead of chewy glue. Unlike thousands of other riders who may have had the same thought, Erickson had the unique skills to pull it off. Although he was living in a garage, Gary was the founder and co-owner of a wholesale baking business and had a full-time job as a plant manager for the bike accessories company Avocet. Thus, he was comfortable with both baking and manufacturing.

Gary and Jay finished their ride that day, which required a stop at a 7-Eleven store where Gary wolfed down a six-pack of mini-donuts in place of the abandoned PowerBar. The next day, Gary called his mother to ask for her help. He asked her if she would donate her time, expertise, and kitchen to help him create a baked energy bar for cycling. It wasn't the first time the two had baked together for profit. Gary's mother had perfected the recipes for Gary's wholesale baking business, Kali's Sweets & Savories. Initially, Gary and his mother tried to rework the PowerBar by starting with its ingredients and modifying them. But they quickly realized that the PowerBar was made with highly processed artificial ingredients. Recreating a tastier version of the PowerBar would have been a chemistry experiment. On the other hand, the cookies that Mrs. Erickson made were delicious, but they were full of butter and sugar—neither healthy nor shelf stable. But the cookie recipe gave them real food as a starting point, so they began there. They substituted natural rice syrup for the butter in the cookie recipe. Oats and dried fruit helped add moisture and texture. Several expensive stand mixers died in the line of duty. Six months later, Gary had a bar he was willing to try out with his cycling buddies. First, though, Erickson had to figure out how to commercially manufacture the energy bars. The bakery business that Gary had founded was too small to produce the bars. Gary and Lisa Thomas (the woman he had hired to help run Kali's Sweets & Savories in Berkeley and to whom he had eventually given a 50 percent stake in that business) found a contract baker to produce the first bars. There were hiccups. Just as in the kitchen, the bar recipe (which was even thicker than cookie dough) was difficult to mix, and the contract baker burned through several motors on their 1,000-pound mixers. The initial packaging was a plain brown wrapper. Gary would take dozens of bars on trips, handing them out to friends to get their feedback. The final recipes were the product of Gary's creativity, his mother's baking skills, and the advice of scores of cyclists.

The last step before launching the product was creating the packaging. Gary set up a meeting with his friend Doug Gilmour. Doug had created the logo for Kali's Sweets & Savories and worked with Gary at Avocet. The pair sat down at Max's Opera Café in San Francisco. As Gary described the bar he had been creating (which he had nicknamed the "synergy bar"), Doug sketched a package on the back of a napkin. He put a climber on a rock face and called it the "Gary Bar." Gary loved the package, but he was reluctant to name the bar after himself. Doug convinced him. As they were finalizing packaging a couple of months later, they ran a trademark search, only to learn that the name might infringe on a product called

Gary's All Natural Peanuts. Erickson wrote a letter to the company, who promptly threatened to sue them. A few days before the bike show where Erickson planned to show the packaged product for the first time, he suddenly thought of using his father's name, Cliff. Even though the package graphic features a climber scaling a cliff, naming the bar after Gary's father had not previously occurred to him. But the bar itself was constructed to tell the story. The following text appears on the back of every Clif Bar:

> Clif Bar is named after my father, Clifford, my childhood hero and companion throughout the Sierra Nevada Mountains.
>
> In 1990, I lived in a garage with my dog, skis, climbing gear, bicycle and two trumpets.
>
> The inspiration to create an energy bar occurred during a day-long, 175-mile bike ride with my buddy Jay. We'd been gnawing on some "other" energy bars all day. Suddenly, despite my hunger, I couldn't take another bite. I thought, "I could make a better bar than this!" That's the moment I now call "the epiphany."
>
> Two years later, after countless hours in Mom's kitchen, the CLIF BAR became a reality. And the mission to create a better-tasting energy bar was accomplished. Thanks, Mom!
>
> —Gary, Owner of Clif Bar Inc.

I am fascinated by the marvelous accident of the Clif Bar's naming. Even though Clif Bar was not the original name for his product, Gary discovered the truth that the name held. He realized the value of the lessons his father had taught him, and how his dad had introduced him to the wilderness. Gary explained the naming in the intro to the story on the back. It's the setup to this story that makes us so willing to accept it, the fact that a successful entrepreneur immediately credits his father for inspiration. This, along with the homemade feeling of the package design—still strikingly similar to Doug Gilmour's original sketch—makes the bar feel like something more than a typical packaged snack.

Bike shops saw it the same way. At the September 1991 bike show, Erickson unveiled the Clif Bar. Rumors were already floating around from the large number of hardcore bikers who had tried Clif Bars while Gary was field-testing them. The interest level was extremely high—over a thousand bike shops said they wanted to sell the bar. The feedback was nearly unanimous, though, that Gary should change the drawing on the front of the package from a climber to a biker. He refused. He knew even then that the bar would need to transcend one sport to be successful, and he felt that the climber symbolized the aspiration he wanted the product to convey. Clif Bar began shipping product in February 1992. Within a month the company sold more Clif Bars than all the cookies and Greek pastries that Kali's had ever produced. The first year, the company grossed $700,000 in sales, jumping to $1.2 million in 1993 and $2.5 million in 1994. Gary Erickson, whose only intention was to create a bar that he would still want to eat after he'd had five, was sitting on a huge hit.

As I head north on U.S. 80, a tank farm and an oil refinery mar the green hillsides just before the bridge crosses the Carquinez straight into Solano County. Then, as I leave the interstate for Route 29, I'm in the suburban sprawl of Vallejo for a few miles, until simply and dramatically, I find myself in the Napa Valley, the finest wine country in the United States. The scenery here slows down considerably. The vineyards begin to appear, one by one on either side of the road. The Mondavi family vineyard is here, with an elegant sign welcoming visitors. The orderly rows of grapes on the vines bud in the springtime as I pass the vineyards—Zinfandel Lane. Every half mile or so there is another vineyard, and I see wine tourists pulling in to sample at nearly every stop. Driving past, I ponder the average blood alcohol level of my fellow motorists.

I reach my goal in St. Helena, where a spa set back from the road conceals a modest office suite. The offices of the Clif Bar Family Winery & Farm are on the second floor, where Gary Erickson greets me with a firm handshake. Erickson is 50, with steel blue eyes commanding a balding head. His energy seems boundless and I scamper down the stairs after him to a casually elegant Italian restaurant where we meet his wife, Kit, for lunch. Kit is an attractive, compact woman with short, wavy brown hair and freckles. Her manner is as direct and uncontrived as Gary's. As we sit outside in the perfect California spring weather, I try to make sense of the journey that led Erickson to found Clif Bar. It's an interesting path because, had you met him in the years before he was a successful entrepreneur, you might never have pegged Erickson for a businessman. And in some ways he is not.

"I was very happy when I lived in the garage," he says, referring to the garage in front of a friend's house where he was living when he created the Clif Bar. "I was racing my bike. I was living hand-to-mouth. I was driving my 1976 Datsun 510 to Yosemite for rock-climbing weekends. I was hanging out with friends. Nothing was missing . . . I didn't start Clif Bar to make money . . . I started Clif Bar because I wanted to make a better energy bar for my friends and myself." Erickson is the supreme example of the accidental entrepreneur.

He was also the supreme example of the outdoor bum. Erickson grew up in Fremont, California, and as a kid worked part-time in a retail sporting-goods store. He spent two years at junior college and finished his degree at California Polytechnic in San Luis Obispo.

Erickson was a fanatic for the outdoors, becoming in turns a dedicated climber and cyclist. His first years out of school were spent doing odd jobs to pay for his outdoor passions.

He worked at a ski shop and spent summers as a mountain guide for Sierra Treks, a wilderness program modeled after Outward Bound. In his third year out of school, Erickson scraped together enough money to take a trip around the world. He skied the Austrian Alps, made an impromptu homestay in Florence, backpacked through France, and went to the village where his grandmother was born in Greece. Then Erickson turned south, heading to the Middle East, India, and Nepal, where he trekked and climbed in the Himalayas.

Erickson returned home enormously depressed about having to resume a normal life. He parked cars for months while he tried to decide what to do with himself. Then, in the spring of 1983, his brother Randy called to ask Gary if he wanted to work in a factory. Randy owned a foundry business, and the bicycle accessories company Avocet had invested in Randy's business. The plan was to make high-end racing seats components and comfortable bike seats. Randy offered Gary the opportunity to sweep floors at a new Avocet manufacturing facility. Gary said yes. Within a few weeks, the person who had been hired to run the new facility had been fired and Randy was left in charge of a huge, empty warehouse and a manufacturing floor with an archaic piece of equipment for manufacturing bike seats. The factory was chronically behind on fulfilling orders, and Gary was pressed into service to get the plant to produce bike saddles faster. The brothers spent their first six months at the factory working 15-hour days to get the plant running on schedule. Gary had known nothing about engineering when he was hired, but now, just to survive, he had to learn how the production equipment worked. He swiftly found he had a knack for machinery. After eight months, Randy went back to

good @ machinery

the foundry and Gary was promoted to plant manager. Within a year, he had gone from sweeping floors to managing 50 employees.

Gary's team at Avocet designed one of the first bicycle seats specifically engineered for a woman. Then, as he became more comfortable with design and materials science, Gary began to innovate. He heard about a gel material that could instantaneously mold itself to the person sitting on it and dampen shocks. It seemed ideal for a bike seat. Unfortunately, the material—from Spenco Gel—was notoriously difficult to work with, and it wasn't considered feasible for a bicycle seat. Gary persisted and developed a manufacturing technique that allowed the process to work, and Avocet began manufacturing the saddle based on his design. It was a huge hit. For the follow-on version of the saddle, Gary learned to use a new technology—CAD/CAM (the first computer-aided design systems)—and the resulting product, the 02 saddle, was later featured in the Museum of Modern Art.

Gary spent a total of eight years at Avocet, but he didn't sit still. While he was with Avocet, Gary started two major endeavors that proved to be critical to his success at Clif Bar. The first was racing bicycles. Gary's work at Avocet had spurred both his knowledge of and interest in bicycles. He had been a rider for a number of years and had completed 16 triathlons in 1985, but his decision to race competitively in 1986 took him into the entirely new world of elite athletes. I talked to Paul McKenzie, the director of Luna Pro Teams (the professional women's cycling team that Clif Bar sponsors), who was a bike enthusiast before he joined Clif Bar as employee number 4. "Gary started a little bit late; he was in his early 30s. When I met him, he was actually an up-and-coming bike racer and I think he aspired to be a professional . . . he was a category 2, which is a very high rating. He had the reputation of being a very strong racer, very competent on the bike. He was also known because he was with Avocet and they were big in the racing industry. He would always be showing up with some new bike saddle to get our opinions." Bike racing gave Erickson an insider position within a large and growing industry with a dedicated fan base, as well as the reputation of being an innovator.

Erickson's second venture in this period was his first entrepreneurial endeavor, Kali's Sweets & Savories. The idea was born in his grandmother's kitchen and named after her. Erickson had grown up eating savory pastries called yohas. Around the same time that he decided to enter bike racing, Gary decided to start a business selling these to bakeries. His mother helped him create a variety of the recipe that could be commercially produced and a variety of fillings. He brought in a friend, Lisa Thomas, to help with the business. Erickson already had a full-time job (in fact, in the eight years Gary worked for Avocet, he never missed a day of production) and knew that he would never be able to keep a baking business going single-handed. The business struggled at first, and Erickson considered closing it after 18 months, when it was turning sales of just $20,000 and losing money. Lisa Thomas was running operations and pressed Erickson to make her a full partner in Kali's. Gary agreed. The business grew, and by the time Erickson started Clif Bar, Kali's (which had added cookies to the yohas) had revenue of $200,000. It never generated a profit, however.

The thing you actually notice when you're sitting with Gary and Kit (assuming you're able to notice anything other than the lusty vapor of butternut squash ravioli washing over you) is how dynamic they are. The couple has unmistakable magnetism, a charisma that is enhanced when they are together. They lean into conversations, engaging physically as well as verbally, and their excitement when talking about the business is palpable. They have the newlyweds' glow, and at first I find it difficult to believe that they have been together for a dozen years. Then, as I talk to them, I'm surprised that they haven't been together for much longer.

Indeed, their relationship may be more of a miracle than Clif Bar itself. Gary first met Kit when Gary was 18, although she doesn't remember this encounter. Then, in college, they met again because both were friends with another student, Elysa. "There was instant chemistry, but I tried to ignore it since she had a boyfriend," he says. A couple of years later, Gary, Elysa, and Kit spent a week climbing together. Gary was smitten when he saw Kit climbing. "She was a dancer and she did ballet on the rock." But Kit was engaged at the time, and Gary restrained himself. Kit remembers this trip vividly: "The three of us went to Yosemite and climbed together. Elysa and I were pestering Gary and giggling and he was right in there with us. He was a great rock climber and a great lead climber. I couldn't help but be attracted to the fun and adventure of it. But I didn't really think of him romantically because I couldn't."

Gary's first real chance to date Kit arrived two years later at an inopportune moment—when he was half a world away in the middle of his yearlong trip around the globe. Elysa wrote him a letter telling him that Kit had broken off her engagement. Gary thought about this for a couple of days, and then wrote Kit a letter revealing his feelings for her. He never sent it. By the time he returned to the United States, Kit had a new boyfriend. This time, she married the man. For the next 14 years, Gary continued a friendship with Kit, never telling her about his feelings. When I ask her about this period, Kit says, "Gary was a close friend. He poured the wine at my wedding. We were very close. But he did say one thing to me when I was married that made me do a double take. We were at a friend's wedding and I was dancing and he said, 'It's so good that you're dancing—I just love to see you dance.' I had never gotten that recognition from the other relationship. Gary knew who I was at a different level. It made me go, 'Whoa!'"

In 1992, near the end of the first year in the life of Clif Bar, Gary got a call from Kit. He rented a cabin year-round in Hope Valley near Lake Tahoe, where the contract bakery for Clif Bar was located, and he had invited Kit and her family to stay over. Kit called to tell Gary that she had separated from her husband and that she and her children badly needed some time away. She asked if the offer to visit the cabin was still open. Gary told her she was welcome to use the place. When she named the dates, Gary said he would be there at the same time, as he spent most weekends skiing in the area during the winter. But he told Kit that there was plenty of room if she wanted to bring the kids up and share the cabin. Kit accepted. Gary panicked, calling all of his friends to get advice. He was 36 years old and still a bachelor. Kit was the only woman Gary ever thought of when the word "marriage" came up. And he had missed a big opportunity the last time he knew she was free. But the verdict was unanimous—it would be unfair to make an advance on Kit while she was vulnerable and going through a divorce. Gary decided to follow the advice.

When Kit arrived with her two children that day, Gary was nervous. After she put the children to bed, the two of them fell into a deep conversation. They discussed the past and the future, Clif Bar and their lives. Kit says, "I wanted to know if he was attached, so I sort of wove it into the conversation. Over the years, I had just become really enamored of him." After several hours of talking, Kit told Gary that she had been thinking about him. She told him that she wanted to explore a relationship together. And within a span of under a year, Gary went from being a 36-year-old bachelor in a garage to a married man living in a mobile home with his new wife and her two children. The story leaves me smiling as I drive out of St. Helena after lunch.

Gary Erickson is a man who knows what he wants and perseveres until he gets it. His patience waiting for Kit is mirrored by his willingness to take huge personal risks for his company. The biggest risk of all was the one he took on April 17, 2000.

That was the day when Gary Erickson almost sold his company. It is an important moment for him, and it's telling that this particular story—not that of the "epiphany ride" where he came up with the idea for the Clif Bar—begins Gary's autobiography, *Raising the Bar*. Erickson's personal narrative is permeated by the implications of the decision he made on that day—the decision to walk away from $60 million.

The 1990s had been good to Clif Bar. When it entered the performance bar segment of the energy bar market in 1992, there was just one other competitor—PowerBar. Balance Bar launched at around the same time as Clif Bar, and the three companies all performed well in a fast-growing market. Clif Bar's sales exploded from $700 thousand in 1992 to $30 million in 1998. To Erickson's surprise, his partner, Lisa Thomas, announced that she wanted to get out of the company that year—either to sell it or be bought out by Gary. He pleaded with her to stay and she took a month-long trip to decide. When she returned, Erickson offered Lisa the opportunity to be the sole CEO of Clif Bar (they had been co-CEOs since the founding of the company). Lisa accepted Gary's offer.

Lisa's reign as sole CEO of Clif Bar was a difficult period in the company's history. Clif Bar had a business culture that was an extension of Erickson's personality, beliefs, and desires. Lisa's style was different. "Gary was the soul of the company," one employee tells me, "That's where the inspiration always came from....There was suddenly this bureaucracy, like we couldn't make a decision." There was also a lot of turnover, the employee says. "People were

suddenly coming and going a lot—not always of their own volition."
One longtime employee, who had worked with Gary closely before
he stepped down, tells me, "Truthfully, you know I don't want to
say horrible things about Lisa, but I just didn't feel like I wanted
to work as hard for her. It wasn't as much fun." Decision-making
slowed down because Lisa was not as decisive as Gary. She had strong
knowledge of the business and understood the vision for Clif Bar, but
even though she and Gary had been partners from the beginning,
it wasn't really her business. A senior Clif Bar employee tells me
simply that "Lisa was an introvert" and the CEO role just wasn't right
for her.

Freed of his daily responsibilities, Erickson poured himself into new
projects, the most important being new products. The company had
done well introducing new flavors of the Clif Bar as well as Clif Shot (a
natural gel that was easier to ingest for elite athletes), but it needed new
products to maintain its growth. One of the complaints about the Clif
Bar was that it was not ideal for women—it had too many calories and
needed more calcium, iron, and folic acid. Erickson inserted himself
into the test kitchen and, in the course of three days, developed four
recipes. (Paul McKenzie puts it more bluntly, saying, "Gary basically
went into the contract bakery, politely pushed everyone aside, and
developed the product himself.") With the help of consumer taste
testers, Gary refined these flavors, and they were the launch flavors
for the new Luna Bar: Nuts Over Chocolate, Lemon Zest, Toasted
Nuts 'n Cranberry, and Chocolate Pecan Pie.

There was a lot of skepticism about Luna. In the same way that the
original Clif Bar seemed very limited because it only talked to serious
endurance athletes like cyclists and climbers, Luna struck many people
(including National Public Radio) as very limiting because of its
focus on women. "Why are they giving up half of the market?" one
analyst mused. But Erickson once again followed his instincts in

pushing the project forward. This is accidental branding at its best. Erickson understood intuitively that to be successful, he needed to build products that superbly met the needs of a defined group of people, not products that did a decent job for everyone. He was unafraid of failure, and by eschewing large promotional spending he reduced the cost of the launch to the point where the company could afford to fail and keep innovating.

When Erickson handed the company to Lisa Thomas, the base business stopped growing. In fact, excluding the sales of Luna, gross revenues in 1999 were down from 1998 for the first time in the company's history. But Erickson had instinctively thrown himself into the area where he could best help Clif Bar. The Luna team predicted a strong launch of $1.5 million in sales for Luna Bar. Actual sales were $10 million and demand exceeded capacity. Luna ultimately became a bigger brand than Clif Bar.

Even though Gary put his passion into helping to develop Luna, he had become detached from the company. He took up golf and tried to stay out of day-to-day decisions to give Lisa a chance to run the show. There was a lot of competition in the industry, and Lisa and other out-siders began telling Erickson that Clif Bar needed to find partners to help grow the business. Mars approached the company in 1999, asking to acquire a minority stake with the option to purchase the rest of the company in five years' time. Erickson agreed to explore the option.

As negotiations with Mars were set to begin, two major transac-tions rocked the industry. First, Kraft acquired Balance Bar. Then Nestlé purchased PowerBar. Suddenly, Clif Bar was competing with two Fortune 100 companies with deep pockets, not a couple of other entrepreneurs. It was terrifying. Business advisers predicted doom—Clif Bar would be outspent and outinvested. Funding was a matter of life and death for the company. In January 2000, Erickson and Thomas agreed to sell Clif Bar. The sale was premium priced at

$120 million—over three times the 1999 revenues of Clif Bar. Gary stood to walk away with $60 million.

Work at Clif Bar came to a near standstill for the next three months as Erickson and Thomas bore down in earnest to sell Clif Bar. "There were suits everywhere," one employee tells me, "which was weird because nobody, I mean nobody, at Clif Bar ever wore a suit." The message went out to the employees that Clif was pursuing a sale because if they didn't do it they would be "squashed." Thomas and Erickson tried to assure people that they would be taken care of, but there was little that they could guarantee.

In February, Thomas and Erickson called a company meeting to announce the sale of Clif Bar. Everyone still in the company today has a crystal clear image of that moment, just as if it were the day Richard Nixon resigned. Kate Torgerson, who had started a little less than two years before, says, "Gary was sitting in the center of the circle, and he was visibly not okay. He said he was going to sell the company. His voice was cracking. I felt like I was getting dumped. It was like getting hit in the chest."

The truth was that Erickson really didn't know what would happen to the company or the people. The acquisition process he'd undergone sounds very similar to what Julie Aigner-Clark had to tell me about her experience. "At first, it's 'We love what you do, we want to you to keep running it.' Then the story changes a bit and by the time you're done, it's all about the money and you know you won't control a single thing the minute the deal is signed."

Gary knew this in his gut when April 17 arrived. And his friends had all told him in no uncertain terms how they felt. Kit had started to cry when he told her, knowing instinctively that Gary would be losing a part of himself. A circle of his friends all refused to buy the concept that Clif Bar couldn't compete. "You have the best products in the industry. You can compete." Even his father was stunned. As the time for the meeting approached, the pressure became unbearable. Gary took a walk. And in the middle of the walk, he realized that he didn't want to sell the company, and that he didn't have to. The most he could lose in a war against Nestlé and Kraft would still leave him with more than he had started with when he lived in a garage. He walked back into the office and told Lisa to send away the bankers.

Lisa was understandably distressed. She had poured all of her efforts for months into the sale. She was exhausted and she wanted security. Her initial reaction was that Erickson needed to give her a nest egg of $10 million in cash in the bank to keep her in the company. Then, a few days later she changed her mind. She resigned as CEO and sent an e-mail out to the company announcing that Gary would be taking over. Then she retreated to think for a week and decided that she wanted Erickson to buy her out of the business. He tried to negotiate a deal with some cash and some equity, but she refused, threatening to dissolve the business if he didn't completely buy her out. Seven months of negotiation through attorneys yielded a settlement that gave Erickson five years to pay Thomas $62 million. It was more than the entire previous year's revenue of Clif Bar. Erickson would need a miracle to pay it off.

I meet Erickson again in his Clif Bar winery office on my second trip to St. Helena. This time, we jump in my rental car to drive to the Erickson house, where we'll meet Kit for dinner. The cool early spring that greeted me on my last trip has disappeared and the mercury hovers near 90 degrees as we turn off the main road. Gary and Kit live in the hills of the Napa Valley. As we wind through a maze of country roads and begin to ascend, we leave the valley floor and enter a forest that has a surprising mix of evergreen and deciduous trees. At the end of a long, twisty road, we enter the Erickson property.

At the base of the long gravel driveway, there are two houses. There is a surprisingly modest two-story house of perhaps 2,000 square feet, and this is where the couple lives. It has a gorgeous view of the Napa Valley from a deck just outside the kitchen, and a nice outdoor grill station, but otherwise I suspect that many of the senior Clif employees live in larger and more impressive dwellings.

A new house under construction sits next to the Erickson house. It is a green design with thick walls, solar panels, and ecofriendly building materials that will allow Gary and Kit to very nearly live off the grid. It is a larger structure than the current house, with some of the extra room put into a guest wing, a motel-style strip of individual rooms for friends and family. Gary is intimately involved in the construction and he walks me around the house, pointing out details about the work and materials. The project is moving slowly, which is unsurprising given his involvement at Clif Bar Inc., the Clif Bar Family Winery & Farm, and the Clif Bar Family Foundation.

Over the years, the family has purchased adjoining lots as they came available for sale, so the entire property is sizable. Gary takes me on a tour of some of the highlights in what looks like a golf cart but feels like an off-road vehicle. It runs on biodiesel, as do the cars that Gary and Kit drive. We stop at the burnt-out remnants of another house, which Gary and Kit acquired after the owners decided not to rebuild. Gary has turned the foundation into a modest party space where he will host the wedding of a family friend. A pool sits nearby, serenely untouched by the conflagration.

Gary still bikes extensively. He has just completed a 60-mile road race in the days before my arrival. The property gives him room to roam, as well as some challenging trails for his mountain bike.

Driving back towards the house, we stop at a barn, where Kit introduces me to some of the other inhabitants of the property. First are the horses. "They're riding horses, but we hardly ever get to ride, so they have a great life spending their days running around the pastures." Then we see the chickens and, after disinfecting my shoes and hands, I step into the nursery and hold a baby chicklet in my hands. I'm not very clear about the imprinting routine that chicks go through after they hatch, but by the way this little guy is looking up at me I think he might actually believe that I'm Mom. The chickens are there to produce eggs and organic chicken for Gary and Kit, and the couple also grows fruit trees (peaches, apples, pears, pluots, and plums), peppers, potatoes, tomatoes, onions, shallots, and corn on the farm and raises turkeys for meat. I also see a couple of pygmy goats but, like the horses, they're just pets. Kit and Gary are far too busy to manage all of this activity themselves (although, as with every other endeavor that they are involved in, they seem to have an unnaturally keen command of the details involved in the farming and animal husbandry), so a caretaker supervises the property and workmen. Still, there is a bucolic air about the farm that makes it hard to believe that it is a working environment.

Back in the house, Gary and I sit on the deck, sipping cool drinks and enjoying some artisanal cheese he brings out. As I watch his two dogs, Vigo (an Australian shepherd) and Sparky (a Norwich terrier) roam about the property below (Vigo seems to have figured out how to disassemble a stone wall), Gary recalls the first days after he called off the sale of Clif Bar, when he started running the company again.

"I told people that I was back and that I was committed, and when they said 'okay,' I sort of took them at face value. In retrospect, I learned that behind the scenes there were pools going on for when I was going to give up. They thought it was a really impulsive decision and they thought I would change my mind when the money would grow. One guy said, 'When they put the right number on the table, you're out.' Two years later, when we were both still there, he changed his mind."

At Clif Bar, there were two reactions to Erickson's return. The old-timers—those who had been with the company for more than two years and knew Gary personally—were relieved. They didn't want to leave Clif Bar or be owned by a corporation. Those that I talked to also felt that Clif Bar had grown to feel too much like any other company during Lisa's reign. Even this group was skeptical, however. They had heard Gary tell them that an acquisition was the only alternative to being crushed by Nestlé and Kraft, and they believed him. Now he was telling them that Clif Bar could make it as a solo company. They were confused.

The second group of people had a larger trust gap, because they had only ever known Lisa as the sole CEO. "We thought, 'Who is this guy?' We just didn't know him at all." This group judged Gary solely by his actions—but in a way that made it easier. He didn't have to repair the damage done to their emotional relationship when he had pulled back from the company or when he decided to sell. He could start with a new relationship. "I didn't know what it meant that he was coming back. Other people told me, 'Gary is so much in this company,' but I didn't see that until later."

Beyond the morale problems at the company, there were serious operational issues. In spite of its success, the company was storing nearly a year's worth of finished-goods inventory for Luna—a product with a shelf life of 11 months. Thomas had outsourced operations in 1999 and cracks were developing in the system. Quality had lagged and threatened to hurt the brand.

Erickson started with the personnel problems and worked outward. There were 65 employees in the company, and he instituted a company-wide meeting every Thursday. He spoke honestly about everything that was going on and in a matter of weeks managed to eliminate the rumor mill that had developed during the sale. He began to sit down with different groups of employees and find out what was making it harder to do their job. "We weren't making much money under Lisa," an employee recalls. "There were things that needed fixing. Gary came in and sat down with everyone that was at an assistant or coordinator level and he asked, 'What do you guys need?' We said, 'We need better dental, vision, to be paid what's fair.' And he immediately fixed that. I have tremendous respect for that." There was also a big difference in the pace of change at Clif Bar under Gary. "Things got done. Fast. If there was something wrong, it didn't stay wrong for long. There wasn't this bureaucracy that we had before. I felt like ideas could happen. When you're in an environment where things don't happen, you get used to it. Then when someone says, 'Let's just do it,' you actually say, 'Wait, we can't do that,' until you realize he's the CEO."

Rebuilding a culture of innovation was one of Gary's key goals. Another longtime employee says, "Gary brought us back to our creative selves." Erickson knew that the only way to survive a fight with huge competitors was to innovate more quickly than their business systems would allow. He had to redevelop the organizational capacity for bold action.

Erickson also worked tirelessly on corporate culture. His archetype for the company—like John Peterman's—was a family. He ran the company through a series of creative exercises to bond them together and make them own the turnaround. He also added more celebration to the experience. Commenting on the company culture during the turnaround, Torgerson says, "My first company party—when I entered the door, Gary's mom was holding plateful of homemade appetizers and personally greeting people. It was that kind of company." The results were spectacular. By 2002 revenue at Clif Bar exceeded

$100 million, and it would double over the five subsequent years. Part of this was the continued explosion of the Luna business, but much of it was due to improved business fundamentals. In 2004, Erickson felt secure enough with the turnaround to promote Sheryl O'Loughlin to CEO to run the company on a daily basis. Erickson's intention was to remain the guiding hand behind O'Loughlin and control the direction of the company.

Kit pops out onto the deck and lets us know that it's time to start dinner. I help her chop up a salad while Gary grills salmon outdoors. Gary and Kit now own 100 percent of Clif Bar and, even counting the debt that exists, they must certainly have a net worth above $500 million. So I am slightly embarrassed to realize that my Manhattan kitchen is larger and slightly better outfitted than theirs. They'll rectify this soon, but it cements my impression that the couple has clear priorities and living off the fat of the land is not one of them.

When we sit down to dinner, the sun is dipping towards the horizon and we're rewarded with a lovely rose-tinged view of the valley. I ask Kit about some of the trees within sight and she identifies a fruitless mulberry tree and some Douglas fir (which I know only as an expensive Christmas tree). As we eat, Kit and Gary begin discussing the new Clif Bar headquarters, which they are about to start constructing. The current Clif facility is a modest building in Berkeley, which the company has outgrown. The new, 100,000-square-foot building in the Alameda Bay area will sit on the water, sport a full restaurant run by a former general manager of Chez Panisse, daycare facilities for employees' children, and a performing arts theatre. Clif Bar will try to secure Leadership in Energy and Environmental Design certification for the building, which will have a grass roof and generate its own energy. The current plans are to locate the restaurant and a bocce ball court atop the roof amidst the greenery.

The move to the new headquarters is scheduled for 2009. Meanwhile, in between my first visit and my second, another big change has taken place in the company—Sheryl has stepped down and Gary and Kit are running daily operations for the company. During our first talk, I had gotten a sense that they might be heading in this direction when Gary had strongly expressed his desire to more directly control the future of Clif Bar. In this iteration, they will be co-CEOs, and if their marriage is any indication, one would think that they will have a seamless partnership.

The move does point to a fundamental challenge for the Accidental Brand, however. Gary has twice stepped back from the CEO role at Clif Bar. Part of this has been situational, but I suspect that part of it comes from Gary's inherent need to keep a close connection to his former life as a cyclist, climber, and traveler. Running a company, particularly one the size Clif Bar has now reached, is a daunting full-time task. While Gary has the will and desire to do it, his interests and activities are very diverse now. In addition to the work being done on the farm, and his need to stay fit and to travel, he and Kit have their charitable interests and a successful winery. To maintain these pursuits while running the business fulltime seems like a stretch.

Most entrepreneurs sell their companies precisely because they arrive at a point where they do not have the right skills to run the business as it expands and because they want to enjoy the fruits of their labors. Erickson does have the skills to run the business, and he did an excellent job of reviving the company after he called off the planned sale. But it is not clear if he has resolved the fundamental tension between his multiple interests and the single-minded focus that the business requires.

I leave the Clif property as dusk subsides into an inky darkness. For a city dweller, the sounds of the forest are surprisingly loud, and

I momentarily panic when my GPS has trouble finding a signal through the tree cover. But soon I am on the road back to San Francisco. Although I will arrive late, the drive through the Napa Valley and back into the city will be 100 miles and eight hours shorter than the ride Gary took a dozen years earlier, the ride he built an empire on.

THE VISIONARY AND THE STRATEGIST: MYRIAM ZAOUI AND ERIC MALKA (THE ART OF SHAVING)

The straight razor catches the light for an instant as the blade angles towards me. I have a thousand things on my mind—the distractions of an average day—but they fade away as I contemplate the perfect edge of that blade and the hand holding it. The hand is not mine. It occurs to me that showing me the razor is an excellent way to get my attention. Not just the subliminal awareness that I have of someone snipping away at my hair with a pair of scissors while I daydream, or even the more deliberate scrutiny I might give a tailor measuring my inseam as the cloth tape ventures into uncomfortable territory. No, the man showing me the business end of a straight razor gets an entirely different kind of respect, the kind I normally reserve for my mother, my accountant, or anyone driving a Ferrari.

The hand in question belongs to the executive master barber for The Art of Shaving. He is about to give me the Royal Shave, the signature treatment of the Miami-based company. The brand, which is now 12 years old, has an ambitious goal—to teach American men how to shave properly. The razor trick is borrowed from the traditional barber shave, an elaborate ritual that has been practiced for centuries. The Art of Shaving has evolved the barber shave into a ceremony that combines elements of performance art, spa treatment, and a skills workshop. Showing me the razor ensures that I'll pay attention to the lesson being given.

It is immediately clear to me that I'm one of the guys who need the company's particular brand of help. Shaving is a lost art in this country. Thanks to the safety razor, anyone can drag a blade across his face without risking major injury. In the process, we've become a nation of abusers, tearing off layers of our skin and submerging hair follicles indiscriminately. When I study myself in the mirror at the handsome The Art of Shaving shop in the upscale Aventura Mall in Miami, I see the results of neglect on my own face as the master barber points them out. Those bumps on my cheek are ingrown hairs—not adult acne—and the blotchy red skin on my neck is razor burn, he explains. I haven't even noticed the razor burn and briefly wonder if I've unconsciously shaved poorly in the days leading up to this experience to give the barber a challenge.

Our national shaving crisis has been amplified by the disappearance of traditional barbers. The 1960s and '70s essentially killed barbering in America. When men began to grow their hair longer, barbers largely refused to cut it. Long, tangled hair required a new set of skills that barbers were reluctant to learn. Shaggy grooming also cut against the grain of the principles of traditional barbering. So barbers revolted. Most refused to master the skill of taming long hair. They dug in their heels and kept snipping the locks and shaving the beards of conservative dressers who dwindled in number as they aged.

At the same time, women's hair stylists had two revelations: they were much better suited than barbers to working on long-haired men, and they were also uniquely effective at selling hair products right from the salon. This made the hairstyling business far more profitable than barbering. As hairstylists blossomed, traditional barbers faded. Yes, you'll still see the telltale candy-cane neon pole in clattertrap old strip malls, but if you look inside a barbershop today you will see mostly older customers and older barbers. "It's such a dying art that we have real problems finding barbers for our shops," the Art of Shaving master barber laments.

In 1996, The Art of Shaving stepped into the gap. This growing empire ($35 million in retail sales in 2007) started as a tiny specialty shop on the Upper East Side of Manhattan. The goal was simple—to help men achieve the perfect shave. Initially, the shop imported the best European shaving products, eventually launching their own line. From the beginning, though, the focus was on education. The company created a shaving system that is the foundation for their business, and it's the one the master barber introduces me to in Miami.

STEP 1: PREPARE

The first step in the perfect shave is preparing the face. The master barber does this in two stages. First, he layers hot towels on my face as if he were swaddling a baby with cloth diapers. The towels cover my eyes, ears, mouth, and nose, leaving just a small hole at the nostrils for me to breathe through. This helps open the pores and softens the beard. "At home, a good time to shave is right after you get out of the

shower—that will give you the same effect," he says. While the heat
of the towels is soothing, the sensory deprivation is not. I suddenly
reconnect with my latent claustrophobia and it transports me back
to my first MRI experience, when I felt like a salted mackerel in a tin
can someone was trying to bang open with a rock. Breathing deeply
through my nostrils helps and I manage to calm myself enough to
enjoy the wet heat from the towels for a few seconds before the master
barber removes them. Then he works his hands down my cheeks and
neck like a dermatologist looking for a malignant mole. "I'm feeling
your beard," he explains, "to see what type of preshave oil your skin
needs." The application of this oil is the second step in preparing
the face for the shave. The Art of Shaving makes preshave oil in
four varieties for sensitive, dry, and oily skin, as well as an unscented
hypoallergenic type. The master barber informs me that my skin is
sensitive, and massages oil with a hint of lavender in it into my face.
The oil forms a protective barrier between my skin and his blade, and
further softens the beard. The oil is also aromatherapy for the face,
formulated with a number of different essential oils. In fact, it was the
idea for this preshave oil that launched the business itself.

Barbers might be the public face of The Art of Shaving, but
the brand is the child of the imagination of Myriam Zaoui and
the entrepreneurial smarts of her husband, Eric Malka. Zaoui and
Malka are immigrants, she from Paris, he from Morocco by way of
Montreal. They strike me as a stylish, confident couple as I meet
them in their corporate offices in Miami. Both are tanned and trim.
Zaoui has a narrow face and a cascade of dark, curly hair that sets off
intense green eyes, while Malka sports a neatly trimmed goatee and
frowns when he thinks. In spite of laboring for more than a decade
to build their business, Zaoui and Malka seem fresh and enthusiastic.
So do their employees, who might pass for cult members if not for
their corporate attire.

In fact, it is the enthusiasm of The Art of Shaving employees that first led me to the brand. I was in Las Vegas at a marketing conference, stranded without toiletries. I'd made the typical devil's bargain of abandoning many of my liquid carry-on items at the airport to avoid checking my bag and losing it. Trial-sized toiletries seem like a good idea, but I've never managed to keep all of the right ones at hand in a clear plastic bag when I need to travel. At an outlet of The Apothecary Shop in the Venetian Resort Hotel Casino, where I was staying, I saw shaving cream and aftershave balm from The Art of Shaving and was immediately drawn to their striking packaging. Later that week, I saw an Art of Shaving retail store in the Fashion Mall just down the Strip and stopped in. The store looked like the lovechild of a Clinique counter and an English barbershop, its dark wood fixtures contrasting smartly with the sleek, clinical-looking product packaging. Elegant display cases housed nickel-plated badger shaving brushes with matching shaving handles, neatly dangling from display stands. As I looked around, it struck me that The Art of Shaving had elevated these obscure shaving artifacts to a new status—they had become objects of desire.

The store clerk, too, was unusual. He knew a lot about shaving and seemed more interested in making sure I understood how to shave properly than he was in selling me shaving balm. I asked him about the origins of the store and he told me about the founders. I immediately knew that I had spotted an Accidental Brand.

Myriam Zaoui had The Art of Shaving's founding idea in her first year with Eric Malka. Zaoui and Malka had met in Miami in late 1994. She was 19 and visiting from Paris, debating whether to take a break from college after studying for two years at the Sorbonne. Eric, who is six years older than Myriam, had just finished his third entrepreneurial endeavor—a mail-order company for prerecorded music that he closed after a year and a half. The pair spent a good deal of time together on her brief trip. When she returned to Miami a few months later, having postponed the rest of her education, Malka wooed her assiduously and the two became a couple.

Seven months later, Malka and Zaoui decided to move to New York together. Eric got a job in finance for a cosmetics distributor importing personal care products from Europe. Myriam, who had worked part-time at a spa equipment manufacturer in Paris while she was in school, found a job on the East Side as an aesthetician doing facials and body treatments at a day spa. She started studying Chinese and ayurvedic herbology through a correspondence certificate program and dabbled in aromatherapy in her spare time.

During this time, Zaoui noticed that Malka would shave at odd hours. Eric suffered from razor burn uncomfortable enough for him to need to shave at night instead of in the morning. Zaoui recalled that, for the same reason, her father would put Johnson's Baby Oil on his skin before using shaving cream. While she wanted to help Malka, the idea of using a mainstream product containing both synthetic mineral oil and artificial ingredients displeased her. She believed that she could formulate something better for the skin and the body using natural and essential oils. Over a period of several months, Zaoui home-brewed a preshave oil that allowed Malka to shave without irritation. It worked beautifully.

[handwritten margin note: started from a personal problem]

STEP 2: LATHER UP!

I sigh audibly as the hot lather glides onto my face. The master barber spreads it quickly so that it fully covers my cheeks and neck before it begins to cool. I am perfectly willing to forgo the shave in return for an application of three or four coats of hot shaving cream. But he insists on continuing with the shave and the lesson. "You can achieve this at home by using a badger brush," he tells me. "You put the shaving cream in the handle of the brush and then drop the brush in steaming hot water. Badger hair is unique in that it retains water. That allows you to get hot lather with the brush." The shaving cream contains glycerin and coconut oil as well as more lavender, and it soothes as it lubricates my beard for the razor.

Zaoui and Malka contemplated starting a business from their very first days together in Miami. Zaoui wanted to open a spa, and the couple went as far as visiting some retail locations before realizing that they couldn't afford the heavy capital investment. After the pair moved to New York in the spring of 1995, the plan reemerged with a twist. Eric's shaving experience had awakened Myriam to a crisis in men's skin care. Women were spending thousands of dollars a year on their skin while men were doing next to nothing. But within the hip confines of downtown Manhattan, a new trend was emerging. Straight men were pampering themselves with expensive personal grooming products in a manner previously seen only in the gay community. In 1994, Mark Simpson coined the term metrosexual to describe these men in an article for the *Independent*. The metrosexual movement was powerful but limited. Although the concept of guys with good skin and trimmed cuticles was novel and played well in major urban centers, the implied androgyny was not palatable to the rest of America. There was just too much sheer femininity inherent in getting manicures and using the high-end facial products that were de rigueur for metrosexuals. Maybe you could get some Wall Street bond broker with more money than sense to get pedicures and use an apricot facial scrub, but you wouldn't catch an accountant from Cleveland dead in a manicurist's, even if he could afford it. Zaoui's innovation—in my opinion the genius insight behind The Art of Shaving as a brand—was to infuse the grooming practices of the metrosexual movement with a deeply masculine flavor taken from traditional English barbering shops by bringing dark wood, an antique barbering chair, and warm tones into The Art of Shaving's first shop.

Visualizing an upscale men's shop is one thing, but actually opening such a store in Manhattan is a completely different proposition. Zaoui and Malka were both under 30. They had no savings and were barely meeting their own expenses while living in a cramped loft in Chelsea. Then, one day in the summer of 1996, while he was on a business trip in London, Zaoui and Malka talked on the phone and she told him she wanted to move forward. "We had enough money to maybe miraculously open a small mom-and-pop shop somewhere," Malka remembers. "After we had the idea to do it, maybe a month passed and Myriam was starting to get cabin fever and she was saying to me, 'So when are we going to start this business you promised me? You said we're going to do it—we're not doing anything.'" Malka told her that, if she wanted to open a shop, she needed to find a location. "I called Myriam from London and she's whining about being bored and she wants to start this business . . . and we're not doing anything to make this business happen. And I literally said to her, 'Listen, you want to open this store, you need to find a location—otherwise we're never going to do it and I'm busy all day with my job. Go out, find a location, then we'll do the store.' I was kind of brushing her off. At that point I had only known her for 18 months—I hadn't seen what she was made of."

It took only a few hours for him to find out. "I had a mission," she says. "I started my walk with 62nd between Lexington and Park and then up block by block to 90th Street and then down between Lexington and Third all the way to 62nd." Her last stop was on 62nd Street between Lexington Avenue and Third Avenue. There was a tiny shop there called Tender Buttons that Myriam admired and that her aunt had introduced her to. She liked the European feel of the store, which featured tens of thousands of antique buttons, and the way it had integrated itself into the neighborhood. As it turned out, a tiny storefront—a former newsstand—was available just a dozen feet from Tender Buttons for $2,600 a month. Eric got a call from her six hours later. She said, "I found the place," and he said, "You're kidding." Malka recalls the moment, saying, "I'm thinking, 'Is she nuts or what? I was just trying to blow her off.'" But Eric was also inspired, and he immediately called the real estate broker for the storefront, who proposed a meeting that afternoon. Eric responded that he was in London and not returning to New York until the next day. "Now this guy thinks I'm an international financier or something, looking for a little business to keep my wife occupied. Needless to say we met him two days later and he was so impressed with us already that he gave us a lease without checking our credit references."

In fact, there was no money in the bank even to sign the lease, which required two months' security and a month of rent upfront. So Eric sold his one remaining possession of value, a snow-white 1993 BMW 325i coupe that he had purchased after seven years of hard work in America. The car netted him $12,000, which left the couple just $5,000 after paying the rent and security deposit to furnish and stock the store. The superintendent in their Chelsea building agreed to build the store out for $1,500. Zaoui was given the remaining $3,500 for furnishings. "I had this vision for the store," she says, and Eric quickly adds, "Myriam described every detail of the store before she set out to go find the furniture, and it is exactly the way it still looks today in all of our locations. The only thing that has changed is our budget to build the stores." To realize the vision on such a small budget, Zaoui complemented finds from flea markets with a few special pieces from a local furniture maker smart enough to see obvious brand name

the long-term opportunity inherent in cutting a new retailer a break. This same mill provides fixtures for all 27 retail stores today.

None of this would have worked if Malka had not been able to stock the store without any upfront cash commitment. As it happened, Malka's employer was more than happy to fill the shelves of the store with European men's shaving products on very generous credit terms. After all, Malka was a gifted finance person, and it made sense that he knew what he was doing opening a shop for his wife in New York.

Zaoui came up with the name "The Art of Shaving" for the store and Eric quickly agreed. Myriam says, "We wanted people walking outside on the street to understand what we were doing from the name because we were one of the only men's shaving shops in the whole country at the time. It was a new concept." To this day, when you see men standing outside an Art of Shaving storefront peering in, they instinctively rub their beards. It is the exact reaction Eric and Myriam were hoping for.

STEP 3: SHAVE

The razor is a wicked little instrument. The blade is disposable for hygienic reasons, and the master barber makes a point of showing me as he replaces it. The silhouette of this modern antiquarian instrument is more angular than the vintage blades in the display case of The Art of Shaving showroom.

I confess to being nervous as the blade touches my face. I grew up in the *Friday the 13th* generation, and pretty much the only place I've ever seen a straight razor is in the hands of some incarnation of Jack the Ripper, so I don't really understand why I should quietly submit to one being scraped along my throat. But my barber has gotten his title for a reason. The blade dances in his hands as he deftly slides it down my exposed neck. The touch is as soft as a whisper—I can actually hear myself being shaved more than feel it. It takes just a moment to realize that I am in the hands of a pro, a guy who wields his straight razor like Michael Shumacher handles a Ferrari. The razor parts the rich shaving lather delicately. It is a pleasurable sensation—a little like having my back scratched—and I find I'm able to relax much more that I would have thought possible.

Oddly, the shave itself is the shortest part of the shaving experience. In fact, I am shaved, relathered, and shaved again in just a few short moments. The lesson here is instructive: if you've done your preparation well, then shaving is quicker and less bloody and offers much better results. Like many of the things The Art of Shaving teaches men, this knowledge is both practical and wise.

My eyes have been closed for most of the shaving experience, but I open them briefly while the razor is doing its work and notice that my shave has attracted a small crowd of onlookers. This surprises me, given that it's before 10:00 A.M. on a Friday morning in the mall. Showcase The barber chair in the Aventura Art of Shaving Store sits in front of two windows very near the food court. Showcasing the barber at work is part of the theater in these mall locations. It is an interesting compromise. It is difficult to imagine anyone wanting to be shaven regularly in front of onlookers. On the other hand, seeing a barber giving a straight-bladed shave in the middle of a mall is arresting and memorable. More than any other single element of the brand, it is the live barbering that distinguishes The Art of Shaving as a business and gives it such a strong feeling of connection with a tradition stored deep in the memory of modern men. This makes the brand authentic in a way that its competitors and retailers alike admire. The expertise that The Art of Shaving radiates also gives it the ability to bring some

combo of traditional and modern technique

distinctly modern innovations to traditional shaving: aromatherapy and herbal medicine. It is this combination of traditional values and spa pampering that made the first Art of Shaving shop unique to Manhattan.

Two weeks before they opened the first store, Zaoui asked Malka, "When are we going to hire someone to run the store?" He just laughed and told her, "That's you. We can't afford anyone else!" The doors opened on the first Art of Shaving store on Sunday, October 6, 1996. The first month was difficult. Zaoui had wanted help in the store not because she was lazy or indifferent but because her English was poor at the time. Helping customers required understanding them, and this was a huge struggle in the first few weeks. On the first day of business, The Art of Shaving store sold a total of $200 and both Zaoui and Malka were ecstatic, even though that number was not near the breakeven level for the store. But soon Zaoui and Malka (who spent his off-work hours in the store) saw a strange phenomenon developing. "People were coming in because they liked the look of the shop and they lived in the neighborhood," Zaoui remembers. "They said, 'Is this a new shop, is it European?' They bought something to support the shop, not because they were really interested at first—even a lot of women buying something for their husbands. Then, all of them, every single one, ended up coming back as a regular customer."

Zaoui and Malka had picked their store location well—it was a neighborhood with enough foot traffic to support retail, and enough community spirit to give a new business a break. It was also—importantly and unexpectedly—one with enough journalists living there to put the store on the map. This was just one of the small decisions—like the choice of dark wood, the name, and the product selections—that marked The Art of Shaving for success as an Accidental Brand.

location was key

A small break came just a week later. A *New York Times* reporter was walking by and stopped in. She asked if The Art of Shaving was a new store, mentioning that she wrote a small column on new businesses in Manhattan. She then wrote a piece in her column on The Art of Shaving that drew enough customers to the store to allow it to break even. The holiday buying season started late during the second month that The Art of Shaving was open. Business bloomed. In the first two months, the store did $10,000 of business each month. In December, its third month, the store grossed $37,000 in sales.

The spectacular increase in sales filled Zaoui and Malka with confidence. In January, barely more than three months after opening the initial store, Malka contacted a real estate broker asking him to find space for another, larger shop on Madison Avenue. Neither 22-year-old Zaoui nor 28-year-old Malka were fazed by the fact that they had only three months' worth of retail experience, no credit history, and no savings. The broker quickly came back with a location on 46th Street and Madison Avenue in the old Roosevelt Hotel, which was undergoing a major renovation. Fortunately for Malka and Zaoui, the Roosevelt didn't have much experience with retail leasing either, and the contract negotiations dragged on for six months. During that time, the business at the Lexington store took a major step forward.

In January 1997, Malka called a barber the couple had met in London and invited him to do a two-day shaving event during his planned trip to the States in February. This barber had cut the hair of British Prime Minister John Major and some of the royal family's lesser members. The Art of Shaving store on Lexington had an antique barber's chair, which was entirely decorative. Zaoui and Malka had decided to make it functional for a couple of days. They wanted to offer complimentary shaves to some of their established customers as a way of sparking more interest in the store.

To promote the event, Zaoui created a simple black-and-white postcard that showed a line drawing of a man receiving a traditional straight razor shave and the words "Complimentary shave by the barber to the Royal Family and Prime Minister of the United Kingdom." Zaoui and Malka sent out 400 of these cards to their customer list. Within three days, an astounding 100 customers had called in to schedule shaves (the normal return rate on postal mailings is less than 2 percent). Malka called back the barber and asked him to make his event at the shop last an entire week, to which the man readily agreed.

One of these postcards found its way into the hands of a young publicist who told Zaoui and Malka that she wanted to work with them. She agreed to promote the shaving event for free to prove her worth to the couple, suggesting that if things went well they could hire her to handle future PR. She was spectacularly successful, landing an article in the Metro section of the Sunday *New York Times* as well as a three-minute piece on CNN, a full-page write-up in *Fortune*, and mentions in *GQ* and other men's magazines. The event was a huge success, and it gave Zaoui and Malka the missing key to making a larger store profitable.

publicity

The Art of Shaving store on Lexington had been selling a variety of shaving accessories, including consumables (shaving cream, aftershave balm, moisturizers, and so on) and hard goods (shaving brushes, razor handles, travel cases). In the ordinary course of business, most of the sales were in consumables. While the barber was in the store, the balance shifted dramatically. Men coming off the chair were spending $300 to $400 and buying a complete shaving system. The barber was able to talk to them about grooming and explain how the different parts of a proper shave interacted—why using a brush is better than one's hands, for instance. Unwittingly, Malka had cracked the code that killed barbershops in the 1970s—he had figured out how to make barbers effective product salespeople. This had also unlocked the key to making a men's grooming store viable—ultimately achieving a register ring averaging nearly $100 per transaction thanks to the increased visibility of hard goods and the presence of a barber.

The *New York Times* piece was published on Sunday, March 23, 1997. Zaoui and Malka, the perfectionist entrepreneurs, zeroed in on the details of the article but completely missed the impact that it would have. "We were looking at it, groaning, and saying 'I don't like the way they did this or this—and this is not cool,'" Malka says with a smile. The next morning, Myriam Zaoui and Eric Malka got married. Eric was already a citizen, but Myriam was in the process of getting her green card. Their immigration lawyer had told them that the laws were changing and that they needed to get married before April 1. Early on the morning of March 24, their witnesses drove them to Great Neck, New York, where the mayor married Eric and Myriam in a short but lovely civil ceremony. They considered closing the store for the day, but Zaoui and Malka had decided they didn't want to be perceived as a "mom and pop" shop and had pledged to each other that they would always keep the store open for its full business hours. So they rushed back into the city with their witnesses and a small wedding cake to open the shop by 10:00 A.M.

Mondays are the slowest days in retail, and Eric and Myriam did not expect to see anyone at the shop before lunchtime. However, according to Eric, ". . . that day as we arrived, there were already people on line waiting to get into the store." The phone was also ringing with people wanting to place orders for the products mentioned in the *Times*. On their wedding day, the store sold over $8,000 and emptied its entire inventory. Eric had to drive to his distribution warehouse that night to get more inventory. The next day was just as crazy, as was each successive day for the next three months. Eric quit his job in June to join The Art of Shaving full-time. He was the second full-time employee.

The *Times* article and the subsequent ramp-up of sales at the Lexington store gave Zaoui and Malka the liquidity they needed to open the flagship store on Madison Avenue. The retail space for that location was far more expensive than the Lexington store—they needed $30,000 just for the security deposit. The experience with the barber event at the Lexington store and its subsequent publicity also convinced Zaoui and Malka to add the "barber spa" as a designed element of the Madison Avenue shop. Myriam still had the ambition of integrating spa treatments and aromatherapy into the traditional barbering experience and saw her chance with the second store. The store opened in August 1997 and with it, The Art of Shaving introduced "The Royal Shave," which surreptitiously added a facial to the classic barber shave. The price point seemed astronomical, but the $45 shave sold exceptionally well. The new store was an instant success. It broke even within two months. This second store, located on one of the premier shopping rows in the world, moved The Art of Shaving into the big time.

STEP 4: MOISTURIZE

The Royal Shave experience that Myriam Zaoui created in New York in 1997 is the same one I am receiving in Miami at the hands of the master barber a decade later. As he finishes shaving me and discards the straight blade, we move to the final element of the shave, which has as many steps as the first three elements combined. It starts with a single hot towel, this one infused with several drops of lemon essential oil. The scent is strong, fresh and invigorating. Then cotton pads are placed on my eyes. These are infused with rosewater, which Zaoui became intimately familiar with in France. The smell is not as cloying and floral as I remember from my grandmother's bathroom, where a bottle of rosewater stood on the sink at night next to her dentures in their glass tumbler. I savor the scent and I am again surprised at Zaoui's ability to reimagine the past.

The next step of the treatment surprises me. My six-foot-three barber begins delicately applying a moisturizing mask to my face. This botanical mask is intended to replace the nutrients the skin loses during the shaving process. It feels cool and comfortable on my face, although I can only imagine what I look like to the teenagers cruising the mall outside the window. Thankfully, he does not place cucumbers on my eyes.

The master barber's name is Michael Felton. Felton is a third-generation barber who grew up on the banks of the Mississippi river in Iowa. His grandfather was an upscale barber at the Blackhawk Hotel in Davenport, where he gave shaves and haircuts to gentlemen disembarking from the grand riverboats that plied the Mississippi. As a child, Felton would sit in his grandfather's shop, watching him practice his art even as the profession disappeared around him.

Felton himself spent years barbering until he left for New York, where he worked steadily in musical theater. That is where The Art of Shaving found him and returned him to his craft. He left the company in 2000 when he decided to return to Iowa to raise children, opening a small shop on the shores of vacation spot Lake Okoboji. I visited Lake Okoboji as a child and remember the bucolic effect of the summer heat on the water. Actually, my strongest memory of the trip was being put at the helm of a pontoon boat—with my parents leaning over the front rail—and almost capsizing the entire craft by hitting the throttle suddenly when all the weight was on the bow. Okoboji has since become a prime, even hip, resort destination, although not as well known as Branson, Missouri.

Felton was reconnected to The Art of Shaving as the chain began to expand past Manhattan. Still based in Iowa, Felton travels extensively for the company, training barbers nationwide and conducting demonstrations and press events. He has made an appearance on *The Martha Stewart Show* several weeks before our meeting, where he demonstrated home shaving techniques for men. "It was great because the national exposure really gave me the opportunity to do more demonstrations and add credibility to my craft," he says. It is clear that Felton's mission, like that of The Art of Shaving, goes well beyond commercial success. He wants to see barbers reassume their rightful place in the lives of American men.

One of the things I am curious about is his opinion of the difference between the straight-bladed razor he has just shaved me with and the multibladed safety razors that most men use on a daily basis. The Art of Shaving stores sell straight-bladed razors, but they are displayed in a way that makes it look to me like they are there more for aesthetic reasons than for sale. Felton confirms this.

"My grandfather shaved people as a practicality. It was a routine for a lot of men to be shaved by a barber. And a barber was more of an expert with a straight-bladed razor than most men could be, so it was safer. But with multibladed safety razors, anyone can get a close shave. We can teach you how to give yourself a much better shave. Especially one that is better for your skin. But getting shaved by a barber these days is a luxury. So this is a pampering treatment." As Felton is talking to me, the store barber—his rank is master barber, just below Felton's rank of executive master barber—arrives for the morning. Felton immediately engages him, drawing him into my experience, "I understand you're one of those rare barbers who has actually been doing this longer than I have," he says.

The barber is from New York, from Queens. He's been drawn to The Art of Shaving because it is literally one of the last places for him to practice his craft in the classic, upscale environment he prefers. "For years, I did women's hair, but I really got fed up with it," he says. After getting divorced and spending a year riding a Harley around the country (I try but fail to imagine this balding, gray-haired man on a lowrider), he heard from a friend about The Art of Shaving.

"I come from a whole family of barbers—my grandfather, my father, my uncles, my cousins—all barbers. But not the kids," the man says.

Felton smiles and nods wistfully. "I've got five boys," he says, "and not one of them is a barber. My wife is pregnant with number six, a girl. She'll probably be my barber."

Felton removes the mask with sponges infused with lemon essential oil. Then he applies a cold towel to my face with more essential oil to close my pores and keep my face from losing moisture. Finally, he applies lavender aftershave balm, tapping it on rather than rubbing it. He explains that the face is sensitive after shaving and that avoiding any pressure there eases discomfort.

"We try to teach customers how to achieve a very close shave in their own home. In three to six months, when your skin is completely healed from all of the things you've done wrong to it, you can routinely go a day without shaving. I shaved yesterday morning but not today, for instance," he says, as I survey his face. He doesn't look unshaven but I am suspicious, thinking he might just have slower-growing facial hair. Of course, Felton towers over me even as I stand, so judging the hairiness of his face is a little like trying to imagine what a postage stamp will look like on an envelope when you're seeing a poster-size version. I imagine that my hairs must be a lot closer together than his.

With this last bit of wisdom, the treatment is over. I shake Felton's hand as he rushes off to another mall to perform a shaving demonstration. I stand in the store for a few moments, slowly stroking my face, marveling at the soft texture of my skin.

I meet Malka and Zaoui for dinner at their waterfront condo in South Miami Beach. Their exclusive building has its own complimentary valet parking for guests, with a stiff fine imposed for "unauthorized valet parking" to discourage tourists. I actually drive around the circular driveway in front of the building twice before I realize that there is indeed guest parking; then I feel like a hick when I awkwardly tip the valet as he takes the keys to the car. The lobby of the building is enormous, modeled after a resort hotel, and I find myself reaching for my credit card to check in at the front desk. Instead, the uniformed attendant checks a list, makes a discreet call, and ushers me to the elevator bank. The elevator I step into has two doors, and the rear door opens directly into Zaoui and Malka's apartment. Zaoui greets me and walks me around a breezy space that looks as if an *Architectural Digest* editor had decorated it. "When we first came here, we brought a lot of our furniture from New York that was more traditional, but it just didn't work. We gradually ended up with everything looking very modern," Zaoui says apologetically.

We sit outside on their balcony at a full-sized dining table with a panoramic view of the city of Miami on one side and Miami Beach and the Atlantic Ocean on the other. Eric joins us after a moment, clad smartly in a lightweight khaki Prada suit. There is a sort of modest elegance about Zaoui and Malka—they have a gorgeous apartment but wouldn't consider splashing out on a boat or a vacation home. They've even hesitated on buying a pied-à-terre in New York, where they now have four stores (including one in the Time Warner Center in Columbus Circle and a new store in Grand Central Terminal). They are energetic but wary, not willing to declare victory when they see their job as less than half done. Not at all what you might expect from the founders and owners of a business that has been doubling in size virtually every year for over a decade.

After the success of the Madison Avenue store, Zaoui and Malka finally had the resources to introduce their own line of men's shaving products to The Art of Shaving stores. The kitchen in their Chelsea apartment became a laboratory as Zaoui worked to formulate the first offerings in a line of aromatherapy-based shaving creams, oils, and lotions. From the first days of the Lexington Avenue store, men had been asking for unscented, hypoallergenic shaving items, which did not exist anywhere on the market at the time. So the first three products to bear The Art of Shaving trademark were unscented pre-shave oil, shaving cream, and aftershave balm. Eric learned Adobe Photoshop to create package labeling, while Myriam perfected her formulations using strictly natural ingredients, including botanical extracts and essential oils. They manufactured a trial run of 1,000 of each of the products. Within a month of being put on the shelves, these became the three top-selling items in both of the couple's stores.

With the success of the first three products, Zaoui and Malka flung themselves full force into developing new products, with 37 new all-natural aromatherapy-based men's shaving products rolling out within the next six months. They created scented lines for normal, dry, and oily skin to complement the unscented line. Most importantly, the products highlighted the philosophy that the couple so passionately believed in: all of the products contain only natural ingredients, including essential oils and herbal extracts to improve health. "Anything you put on your skin ends up in your bloodstream,"

Myriam tells me several times, each time producing a chill. Each time, I also have to ask her to re-explain the difference between an extract and an essential oil. This does not seem to annoy her.

The next big break for The Art of Shaving arrived serendipitously. As Eric and Myriam rolled out the full line of shaving products, Eric made an important contact at Neiman Marcus. An executive for the Dallas-based upscale retail chain had been flying across the country and saw an article on The Art of Shaving Barber Spa and The Royal Shave in the in-flight *American Way* magazine. He thought that it would be a nice idea to open an Art of Shaving Barber Spa in the Neiman Marcus flagship store in downtown Dallas. He called the Madison Avenue store when he landed and reached Eric, who was minding the store alone that evening. They arranged a presentation two weeks later in front of the president of Neiman Marcus. The Nieman Marcus president was a very stern, quiet man who didn't respond much while Eric was giving his pitch.

"After we stopped talking, there was this silence as everyone was waiting to hear what he was going to say. He took this deep breath and then said, 'You don't know this, but my grandfather was a barber.'" The tension in the room broke and a spirited conversation ensued. A year later, in 1999, The Art of Shaving was in the flagship Neiman Marcus store, and the year after that it was established throughout the chain.

Zaoui and Malka invite me to dinner at a restaurant a few minutes' drive from their apartment. I gaze regretfully at the superb view of the setting sun from the terrace as we get up to leave. Malka uses a small remote transmitter to activate the elevator and pushes a button for one of the parking levels. We walk out into a parking garage that seems very ordinary until my eyes adjust to the dim light and I see the cars. This garage could make you think that a Ferrari is an economy car—I count four of them within 50 feet of the elevator. We take Malka's car, a sleek Mercedes CL-550 coupe—a new and limited model with a powerful 400 horsepower engine. The seats have active cooling and massage, and the side bolsters inflate automatically as we move around corners to keep us in place, giving me the strange feeling of being on a theme park ride, like the magic teacups at Disney World. It's a short ride, though, and soon we are sitting in a hushed restaurant, savoring the smell of handmade pasta and garlic.

Malka and Zaoui make an intriguing couple. Malka is more expressive—he is the trained speaker of the pair. He will often finish Zaoui's sentences or interrupt to redirect a thought. Yet I get no sense of irritation from Zaoui—nor do I have the feeling that she is in any way the junior partner in the relationship. Indeed, Zaoui radiates strength and self-assurance. While Eric is the business strategist, real estate genius, and financial wizard, Myriam is the architect of the brand and masterminds packaging, product, and retail execution. When I ask if she is detail-oriented, Eric laughs. "She is the most detail-oriented person that I have ever met," he says, and Myriam agrees. "I am very obsessive," she says, adding that she is fixated on making sure that every single store is absolutely clean and that the merchandising looks right. This is getting much more difficult as the chain opens a new store each month, many modeled on the small but elegant Art of Shaving mall store in Manhattan's Time Warner Center.

Eric is passionate about strategy and growth. He sees the company as a living entity and focuses on the moral and emotional health of the employees. Myriam wants to recreate a vision of the brand she sees in her mind. The retail space, product packaging, and formulations are all attempts to recreate something she has already imagined in precise detail, like a composer who somehow can score an entire opera in her head. In their corporate headquarters, Malka and Zaoui have identically sized offices adjacent to one another. The symbolism is intentional and very clear. They are coequals with different spheres of influence. They complement each other's strengths. And they share the same passion for the business.

By the end of 2000, Eric was ready to return to Miami. Personally, he despised cold weather and longed to live nearer to a year-round beach. Professionally, the distribution of branded Art of Shaving products in Neiman Marcus opened up Eric's eyes to the opportunity for broader wholesale distribution in upscale retailers. This required a larger warehouse and a bigger corporate staff, but expanding their Manhattan headquarters was too expensive. The company could look for suburban space in New Jersey or Westchester or move to another big city.

Zaoui loved New York and did not want to leave. But she especially didn't want to live in the suburbs, and much of her family was in Miami. So in August 2001, Malka and Zaoui secured an apartment, corporate office, and warehouse in the city and began the move.

A month later, as the transition continued, a quiet Tuesday morning was just beginning at their apartment on 29th Street in Manhattan. They had canceled an 8:00 A.M. appointment on Wall Street, and now Myriam ate breakfast while Eric slept. Suddenly Myriam heard a horrendous sound, as if something had crashed into their high-rise. She woke Eric up immediately. Going out onto the balcony, he looked down and saw nothing. Then, scanning the horizon, he saw smoke coming from the World Trade Center.

Myriam turned on the television and soon heard the reports of an airplane hitting one of the buildings. Moments later, it seemed, they heard a roar and a large plane zoomed overhead. Then they heard another crash. The second tower had been hit. An hour later, the towers fell and a wave of smoke and ash rolled up the streets like a tsunami.

Like so many New Yorkers, during the next few days Malka and Zaoui lived through more than they ever expected. They made their apartment a boarding house for stranded employees, with everyone living side by side like a family as they watched events unfold. Zaoui was particularly affected by the thousands of flyers showing the faces of missing loved ones, flyers adorning every building, light pole, and storefront in lower Manhattan. In the first days after September 11, these were pleas for help. Just a few days later, they became a series of vivid obituaries, impossible to avoid for weeks afterward.

Malka ran a high fever for much of the time, his throat aching as he dreamed about the attack. Ten days after the disaster, he and Zaoui rented a car and made the drive to Miami. Malka's body had recovered, but like people across the nation he still felt bereft. "I lost my passion—I really couldn't think about the business." It took half a year to pull himself out of this mood. "One day I woke up and I didn't feel down any more. It was like I was done and ready to get back."

In Miami, Eric and Myriam redoubled their work on the branded product line, with Myriam focusing on the products and Eric on securing more wholesale distribution. Deals with Barneys and Nordstrom followed the successful launch at Neiman Marcus and eventually were joined by distribution at Saks Fifth Avenue and Bloomingdales. The couple began to realize how fortunate the Neiman Marcus placement had been—it gave the brand a sense of exclusivity that made it more appealing to other retailers.

Wholesale distribution came with its own challenges, however. In the couple's Manhattan stores, Myriam could mastermind the retail environment. Every part of the customer experience was controllable and Myriam had a precise plan for all of it. Department stores did not give the brand the same degree of influence. While the brand enjoyed excellent relations with its chain partners, owing to the high register rings that it generated, retailers had the final decision on merchandising issues. But, except in Manhattan, The Art of Shaving had no visible presence outside of these department stores, so the in-store display was even more crucial.

This challenge eventually led Zaoui and Malka to turn back to retail distribution. By opening Art of Shaving stores in malls throughout the country, Malka and Zaoui hoped to maintain control of the brand and further stimulate demand for the branded products at department stores. This led Eric to mastermind a significant retail expansion from Las Vegas (in 2003) to San Francisco (in September 2006). By the end of 2006 the company had 17 stores in full swing. By the end of 2007, the count had reached 27.

About a month after my visit to Miami, Malka and Zaoui are back in New York for a media launch of their new line of women's shaving products. A few days before the launch, I meet Zaoui at 62nd Street and Lexington. She has agreed to show me the original Art of Shaving store. The shop has not changed much in the decade it has been open—the major difference being that The Art of Shaving now produces every single item sold in the store. It is a tiny shop and I am amazed by the creativity evident in shoehorning so much into a cramped space. I can smell the leather of the antique barber's chair, the one that hosted the first barbering event in 1996, as Zaoui shows me the new women's line the couple will be introducing to the media in a few days time. It is not easy to see her in the store as a 22-year-old, struggling with English and uncertain of the store's future. Confidence is her most striking feature, the remarkable ease with which she crafts the stores until every sales item is desirable. As she peers at the positioning of a shaving stand in a display case, her phone rings. It is Malka, who is downtown, preparing for the launch. She smiles slightly as they chat and she waves to me as she leaves the store, ready to continue building their empire.

THE PUGILIST: GERT BOYLE (COLUMBIA SPORTSWEAR)

G ert Boyle is wagging her finger. This is the act for which she is most famous, although her habit of peering stonily at you over the top of her reading glasses ranks a close second. Gert's wagging finger was most recently directed at Microsoft founder Bill Gates, when he asked her whether quality was important at a Windows Vista launch event. The question was a setup, a softball lobbed to the quality-obsessed Boyle, but she smacked it back at Gates. "Quality is not important, it's the *most* important thing," she lectured him, "because once you disappoint a customer, you'll never get them back." Gates sunnily agreed, but you have to wonder whether Gert made him pause for a moment. She has that effect on people.

Thankfully, Gert is not wagging her finger at me. The object of her displeasure is a locked door, or rather the memory behind it. "That was my office. That's where I spent the first 30 years with Columbia. *That* meeting was there."

The office in question is no longer Gert's, or even Columbia Sportswear's, but it is still in the family. The building is now home to the Moonstruck Chocolate Company, owned by Gert's daughter Sally and Sally's husband, David Bany. It is a pretty but unremarkable three-story brick structure surrounded by tall white birch and poplar trees that Gert planted herself in 1957. The building is nestled among a pocket of warehouses and small factories just under the St. John's bridge along the banks of the Willamette River in a blue-collar neighborhood a half hour's drive from downtown Portland, Oregon. Before Moonstruck took over the building in 1996, the place was owned by Columbia Sportswear, the company that Gert helped build—from sales of $800,000 to $500 million during her tenure as president and CEO. It is now a $1.2 billion public company run by her son, Tim Boyle, who has been an employee since his 21st birthday. Gert is still chairman of the board at 83 years of age. These days her duties are mostly centered on publicity, but she still works a 40-hour week and signs every check that the company issues.

That meeting—the one Gert is talking about that transpired behind the locked door in Gert's original office—does a lot to define the company she has built. It took place in the summer of 1971, a year after Gert had accidentally become the CEO of Columbia Sportswear. That was the day she almost sold the company. Had *that* meeting gone as expected, Gert's life would have been completely different.

Columbia Sportswear started life as the Columbia Hat Company in 1938. Gert's father, Paul, had fled Nazi Germany with Gert, her mother, and two sisters that year and settled in Portland, Oregon. Paul was forced to leave a successful shirt factory behind in Germany. After assuming power, the Nazi government prevented Jews from taking more than $20 in cash from the country. This rule kept Jews from taking wealth out of Germany and enriched the Nazi treasury. As a result, Gert's family arrived in America with plentiful furniture and clothing but no liquid assets. Fortunately for Paul, his mother

(Gert's grandmother) had moved to the United States several years before and he was able to borrow money from her. Paul used this small stake to rent a house for the family and buy the Rosenfeld Hat Company, a small retail hat store. He rechristened his new business the Columbia Hat Company—a name that sounded more American to him. This was a time when all respectable men wore hats. Purchasing a hat shop was a safe investment.

Gert was a teenager at the time. She was forcibly integrated into American society when, because of her poor English, the school system placed her in a first grade class with children less than half her age. She worked her way out of the class in just two weeks and joined the seventh grade. Throughout her teenage years, Gert worked in the hat shop on weekends. She left Oregon for college in Arizona, but returned after graduating. She brought a husband—Neal—back to Portland with her and he joined the family business. Gert stayed home to take care of her newborn son, Tim, who was followed by two daughters.

By the 1950s, hats had started to wane in popularity. A major revolution in the apparel business touched this off—the advent of ready-to-wear clothing. Now that technology allowed mass-production of clothes in common sizes, clothing became cheaper and casual dressing proliferated. Fewer of these casual clothing styles complemented hats, and the industry began to decline. Paul and Neal recognized the trend early and began to expand the Columbia Hat Company into other products. Seeing that many of their customers were outdoorsmen, Paul and Neal expanded the hat shop to include outerwear for hunters, fishermen, and skiers. In 1959, after having trouble with a vendor who manufactured ski gloves for the shop, Paul and Neal decided to start manufacturing some of their own products. They created a new business, the Columbia Manufacturing Company. A year later they merged the manufacturing company and the hat store into Columbia Sportswear.

Although Gert was not involved in the business in those years, she did make one important contribution to Columbia in the early 1960s. In those days, fly-fishing required carrying heavy tackle boxes into the river. One day Neal came home from work buzzing with an idea a customer had put into his head. The customer, after seeing a vest with multiple pockets from another manufacturer, had asked if Columbia would be making a fishing vest. Neal wanted to know if Gert could sew a vest with enough pockets to carry the hooks, lures, spinners, flies, bait, and tackle that an angler would need, freeing him to leave the box on shore. Gert spent several weeks sewing furiously, getting input from Neal and some friends as she progressed. She added some innovations like a magnet to hold flies and lures outside of a pocket and a curtain hook to hold the rod while the angler tied flies.

The Columbia Sportswear fishing vest became the best-selling item in the small company's history. It taught both Neal and Gert that there was opportunity in listening to the customer and designing products that uniquely met their needs. It also established the niche that Columbia would successfully turn into a billion-dollar business—taking existing products and making them more usable and tougher, then selling them at a reasonable price. The fishing vest innovation was followed by raingear that became renowned for its strength and durability. Columbia started selling to more and more retailers, and soon Paul and Neal purchased a new building to house manufacturing, a warehouse, and the corporate offices. The building had been a maraschino cherry cannery, and Gert's son Tim spent his adolescent years washing the cherry smell off the floors and walls of the factory.

In 1964, Gert's father, Paul, suffered a stroke. He died shortly after in the hospital. At the age of 38, Neal took over the business, which was grossing $400,000 annually. Gert's mother became the CFO, deciding that she wanted to control her financial future by signing every check that the business issued. Over the next half-dozen years, Neal aggressively expanded the business, hiring more salespeople and dramatically increasing the number of products Columbia sold.

By 1970, Columbia Sportswear had reached a comfortable place. It was a small but respected manufacturer for anglers, skiers, and hunters. The business was profitable, although only marginally so. Neal had plans for expansion and had secured a $150,000 Small Business Administration loan, secured by their house and by Gert's family house, where her mother still lived. Gert's son Tim was in his last year of college and got married in November 1970. Although Gert and Neal were not wealthy people, they could pay their bills. Prosperity seemed inevitable.

But on the morning of December 4, 1970, everything changed. Neal was getting ready for work when he starting feeling pain in his chest. He had been healthy his entire life (his worst adult malady had been hay fever), so he tried to ignore it. When the pain got more severe, he told Gert to call the family doctor. The doctor told Gert to take Neal to the emergency room. She bundled Neal and her 12-year-old daughter Sally into the back of their red Mustang convertible and sped off, but Neal died just moments later in the car. He was 47.

Three days later, Gert Boyle became president and CEO of the Columbia Sportswear Company. She had spent the past 22 years of her life as a mother and housewife and had never held down a full-time job. Tim took the day off of school and joined her. Gert told the employees that the company would keep going and that she'd need their help.

Gert's first year as a CEO was a disaster from the first day. Within the first month, she had to conduct an annual inventory. An employee offered to take Neal's place but demanded that her salary be doubled. Gert gave the woman her raise but then fired her a few weeks after the inventory was completed. Even though Gert had neither the training nor experience to run the company, she was determined not to let anyone take advantage of her. Tim abandoned his plans for a career in law and came to work with Gert full-time just after graduating college at the University of Oregon. He was 21. When I ask him about making this difficult choice, he says, "The business had a negative net worth of about $450,000. My mom's and grandmother's houses were pledged against the SBA loan. If the business failed, my family would have been ruined. There was no choice."

Compounding Gert's grief was her growing awareness of the inadequacies of her deceased husband, Neal, as a business manager. Neal had been a micromanager, personally directing the daily efforts of virtually all of the Columbia Sportswear employees. Many of these people were unused to doing their job without close direction. Neal had also expanded the business chaotically. Columbia was producing hundreds of products, many of them not profitable. Neal was not a saver, and the company was operating from a delicate cash position. Suppliers were understandably reluctant to extend credit to Neal's inexperienced widow, and this immediately put Columbia in a predicament. Without cash, Columbia could not purchase cloth and other raw materials to manufacture into finished products. Without products, Columbia could not generate revenue to pay for more raw materials. Sales in the first 12 months of Gert's reign at Columbia dropped by over 25 percent.

Within the year, Gert decided that she would have to sell the business. She did not have the experience to run the company, and vendors, retailers, and employees alike were taking advantage of her. Sales declined from $800,000 to $600,000, and Columbia Sportswear's bankers threatened to withdraw their line of credit if Gert did not explore a sale. The bank agreed to help Columbia locate a buyer and soon they had found a good match, a local executive with garment industry experience who made a reasonable bid for Columbia. "Reasonable," to Gert, meant that she'd be able to get out from under the SBA and bank loans and walk away with enough cash to give her a few months to find a job to support herself and her youngest daughter, Sally.

The office I am standing in front of—the one Gert has been wagging her finger at—is where the final meeting with this prospective buyer took place. He was in the company offices to conclude the purchase. Instead of signing the contract, however, he surprised Gert by beginning to renegotiate the terms of the agreement. "I don't want the entire zipper inventory . . . I don't want to buy this entire building," he said as he began to itemize a list of deductions to the purchase price. Initially stunned, Gert finally started to calculate the effect of these deductions on the purchase price of the company. She was shocked to realize that this man expected her to turn over Columbia Sportswear for a net sum of just $1,400. True, she would be clear of the debts of the company, but she still knew that the business was worth more.

So Gert did what she does best. She gave the man a piece of her mind—in colorful, highly descriptive language. Her tirade ended with the statement, "For that price, I can run this company into the ground myself," and her wagging finger was pointing to the door of her office. Instead of selling Columbia Sportswear, Gert Boyle all but physically ejected the prospective buyer from the premises.

It takes some imagination to make the leap from the door of this office in 2007 back to the same place in 1971. For one thing, the building has been beautified by Moonstruck Chocolates. They've hollowed out the structure by removing sections of the ground and second floors, creating a dramatic view of the production area (down in the basement) that can be seen all the way from the executive conference room on the second floor of the building. The furniture is still utilitarian, but it's far more stylish than what existed nearly 40 years ago. And Moonstruck is a media darling, a cheerful, successful company that is growing by leaps and bounds. It doesn't have the air of desperation that must have hung like a shroud over Columbia Sportswear at the end of 1971.

Gert Boyle emerged from the abortive sale of Columbia Sportswear a changed woman. Having been shamed by an arrogant man trying to take advantage of her, she was determined to succeed. Her bankers, seeing a spark of life in her that they had not previously detected, agreed to extend the company's line of credit for six months. The bank also offered to put together a board of advisers for the company, and Gert—who had been stubborn about accepting advice for the past year—readily agreed. It turned out that the bank was also lending funds to a start-up shoe company in Beaverton, and within weeks Gert had a senior executive from Nike on her board. The board gave Gert an important piece of advice by suggesting that Columbia's product offering was far too broad. They pointed out that many of the products Columbia produced were "me too" items that were made just as well by other manufacturers. They suggested dramatically slimming the product offering to focus on the items where Columbia's offerings were unique. Gert took the advice. The last catalog that Columbia Sportswear produced under Neal Boyle was 40 pages long and featured everything from baseball bats to rain gear. After retooling the company, Gert produced a catalog that was just 12 pages long and had less than half the number of items. She focused on items that sold well and those that were unique to Columbia, like the fisherman's vest she had designed a decade earlier.

Narrowing the product offerings allowed Gert to slim down the company. Gert saw that expenses were too high and many people were not contributing. She fired over a third of Columbia's employees—both the incompetents and those who had never accepted her as a replacement for her husband, Neal. She later learned that one of these people had been colluding with the man who had tried to buy the company, supplying him with detailed information on inventory, sales, and employee morale. Then she lined up the rest of the employees and told them, "We're going to run this business. We almost sold it but we're here to stay. If you're with us, we will be loyal to you." The mood inside the company began to change. Instead of seeing a short, overweight housewife, employees began to understand the character of the person inside Gert Boyle.

The changes at Columbia started to pay off, as did Gert's attention to detail. Trained by her mother as a seamstress, Gert had been working shifts in the factory since the week after Neal's death. For a period of time, she and Tim were the entire night shift, alternating nights between them so that one of them could watch Sally. "Every night I was saying to myself, 'Oh my God, please don't let the thread break on the surger.' You know what a surger is? It loops the material over so it doesn't fray. I didn't know how to thread it." Sewing the garments gave Gert an unusually keen understanding of their construction and the weaknesses in their design. She wasn't a sportsman and, unlike Gary Erickson at Clif Bar or most of the other entrepreneurs in this book, she was not the core user of her own product. But she had a Depression-era mentality about value and she did not believe that high quality and low price were incompatible goals. Gert could not abide overpriced products any more than she could tolerate shoddily sewn or poorly designed garments, and she wasn't interested in making them. She knew her garments down to the last stitch. Gert also knew she wasn't the expert on what would make them better. So she asked her customers.

Just like Stew Leonard's, the famous dairy store in Connecticut, Columbia Sportswear began gathering groups of its best customers to get input on their products. In Columbia's case, however, these customers were retail store owners. The owners of retail sporting-goods stores shared the same outdoor passions as their customers. They knew both the sports and their customers' needs. Gert systematically built these sportsmen into the design process. The strategy had two benefits for Columbia: it gave the company the accumulated wisdom of the thousands of consumers that each retailer was selling to—a wealth of personal insights honed by years in the field—and it gave the retailers more of an emotional stake in Columbia's business because they had helped design the products.

Focusing on fewer products, ones that offered real innovation, paid off for Columbia Sportswear and the company began to expand. By the mid-1970s, the business was several times larger than it had been under Neal and the threat of bankruptcy had receded. The business strategy had also crystallized. Columbia still focused on outerwear for skiers, hunters, and anglers. Within the category, however, Columbia would be known for well-designed, durable, innovative products sold at a value price. It was a brilliant strategy because it exploded the myth concocted by the high end of the market—that quality means cost because "you get what you pay for." Gert thought that some people were paying too much for overdesigned products.

Columbia's success in implementing this high-value/low-price strategy depended on the tricky act of simultaneously keeping quality high and costs low. Gert did this by working on the factory floor, to ensure she had her finger on the pulse of production, and by signing all of the checks in the company, as her mother used to do to keep control of spending. Tim increasingly focused on sales and distribution. He attended the trade shows alone, without Gert. "I never went to a show with Tim because the last thing you need is to have your mother trailing around behind you, looking over your shoulder," she says. Early on, Tim caught a break from a luminary in the ski industry, Harold Hirsch from White Stag. Hirsch had known Tim's father, Neal, and he took an interest in Tim's welfare. "Harold was 'Mr. Ski,'" Gert says. "He really knew everything about that industry. He knew the story, knew what had happened to my husband, and he took Tim under his wing." White Stag was one of the largest ski outerwear manufacturers at the time, and Hirsch's visible support of Tim gave confidence to retailers, who soon expanded distribution of Columbia's products. With a strong stable of basic products and retailer support, Columbia was only missing a breakaway hit to become a top-tier brand. It came in the early 1980s.

It was actually skiwear that finally put Columbia on the map as a world-class brand. Columbia brought a concept to hunting— integrated layering. Instead of combining insulation and water resistance into a single garment, a layered system allowed the user to adjust the parka for different weather conditions. A few high-end brands were selling layered ski systems at the time, but these cost over $250. In 1982, Columbia introduced the Quad Parka, which were as durable as the existing ski layering systems but featured a better ergonomic design for just $100. The success of the Quad Parka freed up cash for a television ad campaign. It also set the stage for the company's first breakaway product success.

Gert drives us in her BMW X-5 from the old factory to the new headquarters of Columbia Sportswear, on the outskirts of Portland.

The company moved in 2002 when it had outgrown not only the original plant building but also the entire neighborhood. For a number of years, Columbia had been acquiring buildings near the original building to provide extra production, warehousing, and distribution space. But the company kept growing and needed better road access than the old neighborhood could provide. When Columbia moved, it split its facilities between distribution (in the form of an enormous automated distribution center a half hour's drive from Portland) and corporate offices. The new corporate office is an attractive building sitting in front of a duck pond with a sign saying "Welcome to Ma Boyle Country" in front of the parking lot. Walking into the building, I see the original safe from the Rosenfeld Hat Company sitting behind the main reception desk. Gert tells me she still uses the safe to store important documents. The atmosphere is open and cheerful, as are the employees. Everywhere I turn, there is a picture or image of Gert.

In fact, by the time we get to Gert's office, I have seen Gert staring down at me more than a dozen times. Her stern, lined face is an odd contrast to the breezy, open office plan at Columbia Sportswear, where a legion of abnormally healthy-looking young men and women bounce around with garment samples in their hands. Seeing a poster-sized blowup of a print ad featuring Gert—she's shot from below, with a stormy sky and gnarled oak branch looming over her, and the headline says, "Stay as Warm and Dry as Her Pot Roast"—I get a sudden flashback to a statue park I once visited outside of Budapest in Hungary, a site where relics of the Cold War have found a permanent home. Gert's foreboding face reminds me of the enormous monuments of communist leaders like Stalin and Lenin, possessing supernatural strength and vitality. The effect at Columbia Sportswear is more benign but not entirely different. When you work at Columbia, you are always under Gert's eye, directly or indirectly. In the 1970s, this was literally true. Gert was omnipresent; from the factory floor to the warehouse and on up to the management offices. Now it is figuratively true. Columbia has made a conscious choice to use Gert as a symbol of its core values (which, for the record, are Outdoor, Active, Authentic, American, and Value.) When you are working for Columbia and you see Gert's face looking down at you over those horn-rimmed reading glasses, you ask yourself whether you've designed a product that will last and whether you spent a dollar you didn't have to in the process.

This cult of personality was not given a marketing voice until 1984. That's when the first television advertising campaign for Columbia Sportswear launched. The campaign, which has survived in various iterations for more than a generation, is one of the most iconic ad campaigns of the twentieth century. The theme in all of these spots is the same—Gert abusing her hapless son Tim in order to test the ruggedness of Columbia sportswear products. Over the course of the advertising campaign, Tim has been shoved outside in every manner of inclement weather, buried under an ice-skating rink and run over by a Zamboni (driven by Gert), run through a carwash, blow-darted, and abandoned in the Yukon.

funny ads

The creators of the campaign are the two founders of the small Portland-based advertising agency, Borders Perrin Norrander. Account director Wes Perrin and creative director Bill Borders are both retired from the agency, though Borders has left Portland for Montana. The agency had been hired by Tim in the late 1970s to create a new logo for Columbia Sportswear. Then, in the early 1980s, they did some very limited print advertising around the theme "We don't design it—we engineer it." By 1983, Columbia had the means to advertise more aggressively and the desire to build interest in a new system of layered, interconnected garments.

The model for the new campaign was the Perdue ads featuring Frank Purdue and the tagline "It takes a tough man to make a tender chicken." Borders and Perrin figured that showing a tough founder for a sportswear company would make more sense. And Gert Boyle was one tough founder. "The first time we went in to meet Tim, Gert popped in. She was down the hall and saw us come in. She wanted to know what was going on. We found out that you dealt with Gert whether you wanted to or not—she was part of the conversation." The partners realized that, within the entire sportswear industry, the interplay between Gert and Tim was unique. They wanted to put a human face on the company, to show it was a family-run enterprise, but they needed to do so without compromising the premise that Columbia Sportswear was ruthlessly dedicated to quality. In Gert Boyle, Borders and Perrin found their solution.

Gert was reluctant to become the star of Columbia's advertising. She didn't see herself as a TV star and had no acting experience. It was Tim who immediately grasped the most compelling argument that might convince Gert to cooperate—that, by starring in the commercials, Gert and Tim would avoid having to pay any talent fees for the advertising campaign. The advertising had an immediate impact on the Columbia Sportswear business. The brand exploded as sales increased 44 percent per year (figured by compounded annual growth rate) in the five years after the launch of the campaign. The advertising was extremely persuasive. Once people understood that a mother who was the world's most demanding boss ran Columbia, they believed that the products could be both tough and inexpensive. Gert Boyle herself came to epitomize both tough and cheap.

The advertising also transformed Gert into an icon and effectively launched the cult of personality that exists today at Columbia Sportswear headquarters. In one ad, Gert is shown with a posse of bikers and sports a tattoo on her shoulder that says, "Born to Nag." To this day, people that Gert meets, including celebrities, ask her if they can see this tattoo. Gert tells them, "You're not going to find out on the first date!" (She is quick to let me know that the tattoo was temporary.) When I ask Gert about the most enjoyable part of the success of Columbia Sportswear, she unhesitatingly says, "It's not the money. Money doesn't make you happy, it just allows you to suffer in comfort. It's the recognition. There weren't any women running sportswear companies when I started and it's nice to be recognized for doing this." Gert clearly enjoys the attention that the advertising campaign has brought and she revels in the role of being the senior statesman for the company.

The more time I spend inside Columbia Sportswear, the more I am intrigued by her role within the culture. Gert Boyle never got an MBA, never had management training, and never worked for anyone but herself in her life. So the decisions she made were intuitive, based on her instincts, values, and judgment. Gert, like most of the entrepreneurs described in this book, is a demanding, detail-oriented perfectionist. Her greatest source of experience was as a mother. And thus, her management style could rightly be called "motherly" as well.

At 83 years old, Gert Boyle is one of the first employees to arrive at Columbia Sportswear in the morning. She shows up to work every day and puts in a full day. Gert stepped down as CEO in 1989, giving the mantle to Tim, and most of her duties these days are related to publicity. She travels widely—she was in Panama for a store opening the week before I see her, and a month later she'll be in Austria. One of her ongoing duties, however, brings her in direct contact with nearly everyone in the company at some point. I am visiting Columbia Sportswear on a Wednesday, and it is on Wednesdays that Gert signs checks. Throughout the day she continues this task when she is not with me, and several times I hear pages asking people to report to her office. I ask Doug Prentice, the VP of Innovation for Columbia, about the pages. "She's calling people to ask about their expense reports," he laughs, adding, "She has this uncanny ability to know when someone is trying to sneak something by her."

Prentice recalls the case of Dave Robinson, who was hired to head sales for the hunting and fishing businesses at Columbia. Dave was a passionate hunter and often took his key customers on hunting trips. On one occasion, Dave took a group out for a duck hunt. The weather was rainy, cold, and nasty, perfect for showing off Columbia's rain gear. Days after returning from his trip, Dave received a peremptory page from Gert. Arriving in her office with Doug (his boss at the time), Dave was left standing as Gert scrutinized a long grocery store receipt from his trip. In spite of a lifetime spent armed and tracking animals, Dave was literally shaking in his boots. Gert looked up at him, peering over those glasses, and said, "Just what is the meaning of this?" Dave shook his head, uncomprehending. "This!" Gert insisted and wagged her finger at the grocery store receipt for the trip. "I am not paying for your pleasures!" she boomed. Dave looked closely at the bill and then turned deep red. Gert was pointing to a line on the receipt that showed a charge for $5 for two boxes of condoms. He took a moment to compose himself, then spoke. "You put them over the gun barrels to keep the mud out when you're hunting and it's wet," he stammered. Satisfied, Gert nodded briskly and shooed him away.

It's easy to draw a stereotype of Gert Boyle as a tough boss. But Gert isn't known simply for terrorizing employees—a quality that in and of itself would not distinguish her from scores of more traditional corporate executives, from Michael Eisner to Bob Nardelli. There is another side to the persona that she created for the company, one that Prentice explains with a single anecdote. "I was all of 29 years old when I started here. I moved from Minneapolis. I had a wife and a dog, and for the first six weeks I had to commute from Minneapolis to Portland until they could move out. After the first two weeks, Gert asked me where I was staying. She had a trip planned out of town for a few weeks, so she gave me the keys to her house. 'There's no sense in paying for a motel. I'm not going to be there, just use my house,' she says. And for 10 days, I stayed in her house. It was the house that Tim had grown up in—I stayed in his room. I had been working for the company for less than a month. The trust was there, immediately."

Gert wasn't building a company so much as a family. Customers were part of it as well as employees. She was a stern mother, but she was also fair. She was very clear about her principles ("Gert would always challenge us about value," one employee says, "she was always concerned if we were giving a good value to the consumer.") and she was very, very consistent. But the real person behind the myth is much more approachable—and funnier—than first impressions would suggest. When I ask Gert if I can record her, she immediately says, "Of course you can. Just take out the swear words unless you spell 'em right!" She continues with that sort of easy banter for most of the day.

On the advertising shoots as well, her humor and energy became legendary. Dan Hanson, the VP of marketing, recalls a shoot that ran through the night, with the only shelter being inside an old cabin—a frontier-era bordello. At 4 A.M., everyone was nodding off, waiting for the director to set up a shot. "Gert was yakking away like it was the middle of the afternoon. We were all just like, 'Please, let us sleep!'"

In 1986, Columbia created a new ski system featuring brighter, co-ordinated colors, offerings for women, and a better name—Bugaboo. Bugaboo—like its predecessor, the Quad Parka—was designed as a set of interchangeable layers, but it was more stylish, innovative, and appealing. More importantly, it was for skiers—a rapidly growing market. The Bugaboo proved to be the biggest hit in the history of Columbia Sportswear. In the same year, Gert (at the age of 65) stepped down as CEO and passed the mantle to Tim. Gert became chairman of the board, the post she still holds today.

We have lunch in a conference room at Columbia Sportswear. Sandwiches are ordered in and we keep working through the meal, as Gert is prone to do. I ask her about the progress on signing checks for the day. "I only have two today that I didn't sign," she says happily. I wonder again how it is that a $1.2 billion public company can possibly have one person signing every paycheck, expense check, and vendor payment check. It occurs to me for the first time that each one of those employees and suppliers is reminded of Gert Boyle's values each time they cash a check.

The most intriguing dynamic in Columbia Sportswear is the relationship between Gert and Tim. Over half of the Accidental Brands in this book involve family efforts, but most of these are husband-wife pairs. The Art of Shaving and Baby Einstein had the husbands joining their wives' businesses full-time within a year of founding. John Peterman's wife, Audrey, ran customer service for J. Peterman, and Clif Bar founder Gary Erickson's wife, Kit, has become increasingly involved as time has gone on, now effectively acting as a co-CEO. Columbia Sportswear is unique in featuring a mother-son duo. As Gert says succinctly, "If a young man works with his father, everyone says, 'Isn't that wonderful!' But if he works with his mother, people say, 'Oh my God, how can you stand it?'"

I ask both Gert and Tim separately about working with each other, and their answers are remarkably close. "It's not gotten any easier," Tim laughs. "Working with your family members has a lot of interpersonal dynamics. As the business has progressed, we gravitated to areas where we don't bump into each other very much." Gert says nearly the same thing, adding, "When you work with your family, they know your Achilles' heel, they know how to get to you. That can be difficult." As the company has grown, their spheres have grown increasingly distinct. Long gone are the days when Gert might overhear the advertising agency talking to Tim in his office and unexpectedly pop in on the meeting. In the new headquarters building, Gert and Tim's offices are on opposite ends from each other.

Gert still lives in Portland, although she is now in a new house up the hill from the one where she raised Tim. She lives alone except for a butler named Charlie who is, in fact, a mannequin. Charlie's role is largely confined to standing in the window, one arm lifted in a perpetual wave to the neighborhood children. Gert has never remarried and for the past 37 years seems to have regarded dating more as a topic for humor than a pastime for a widowed woman. Columbia Sportswear is her family, and Gert still spends her days with her family. More of her energy is focused on community outreach and charity than it was during the early days, when survival seemed unlikely, but she is otherwise largely unchanged. Most importantly, she continues to imbue her company with the spirit that made it successful. Columbia Sportswear has an eternal chip on its shoulder—it may now be the giant in its industry, but it always must do more for less than its competitors, many of whom sell products at a substantial premium to Columbia Sportswear. As I prepare to leave, Gert gives me a smile and shakes my hand firmly. She invites me to visit again when I am in town. She will surely be there, minding the store and watching over her family.

THE PERFECTIONIST: JULIE AIGNER-CLARK (BABY EINSTEIN)

> Our one-year-old son had gone to bed and we started talking about Baby Einstein. We had two couples over who didn't have children and they didn't understand why it was such a big deal. But kids are just amazed by it. So we pulled out the video and showed it to them, and then another. Then we realized that six adults had just spent over an hour watching baby videos.
>
> —Mark Klienman, Philadelphia

My first glimpse of Julie Clark comes unexpectedly on television. I am watching the State of the Union address. It's the sixth year of George W. Bush's presidency and things are not going well. As a result, the speech lacks the jaunty, boisterous tone that entertains me whether or not I voted for the guy on my screen. The president meanders through the economy, education, health care, immigration, and energy in the first 40 minutes of the address. Just as I am about to flip to a rerun of *CSI,* he begins talking about the contributions of individual Americans who are sitting in the box with the first lady, Laura Bush. This part of the speech is akin to human-interest report on the local evening news ("Fireman Saves Cat From Tree—Cat's Owner Marries Fireman—Story at 11!!") and it perks me up. President Bush first singles out Dikembe Mutombo, the famous Congolese NBA basketball player who has recently donated $15 million for the completion of the Biamba Marie Mutombo Teaching Hospital near Kinshasa, the first modern medical facility in the Congo. Then he introduces Julie Aigner-Clark, saying:

> After her daughter was born, Julie Aigner-Clark searched for ways to share her love of music and art with her child. So, she borrowed some equipment, and began filming children's videos in her basement. The Baby Einstein Company was born—and in just five years her business grew to more than $20 million in sales. In November 2001, Julie sold Baby Einstein to the Walt Disney Company, and with her help Baby Einstein has grown into a $200 million business. Julie represents the great enterprising spirit of America. And she is using her success to help others—producing child safety videos with John Walsh of the National Center for Missing and Exploited Children. Julie says of her new project: "I believe it's the most important thing that I've ever done. I believe that children have the right to live in a world that is safe." So tonight, we are pleased to welcome this talented business entrepreneur and generous social entrepreneur.

Clark is an attractive blond woman with straight hair and frosted lipstick. Her teenage daughter Aspen sits next to her, just behind the first lady. In addition to Mutombo, Clark is surrounded by Wesley

Autrey, a man who recently threw himself in front of an oncoming subway in New York to save the life of a stranger, and Tommy Rieman, a U.S. Army sergeant who has been awarded the Silver Star for bravery under fire in Iraq.

"It came as a complete surprise," Clark tells me later, "and it was this huge secret, so I couldn't tell anyone until literally moments before it happened." What was she thinking while she was sitting there and wondering if the president might mention her among the dozen or so people sitting in the first lady's box? "The whole time during the speech I was . . . Well, as a mother of a teenager, all I could do is keep poking Aspen and whispering 'Don't pick your nose, quit pulling your hair, stop touching your knee—don't kick the first lady in the head!'"

Clark's appearance in the State of the Union address creates some controversy. The next day Timothy Noah, writing for the Web zine *Slate,* titles his account "Bush's Baby Einstein Gaffe—The President Lionizes a Mountebank." He argues that Clark is a charlatan who has defrauded other women with the videos by playing on their neuroses. Clark is surprised by the attack and, like other entrepreneurs I've encountered, she is particularly vulnerable and thin-skinned. "I was upset—I guess it was because I was being attacked really personally by someone who didn't know anything about me. The fact that he totally neglected to mention anything about The Safe Side really annoyed me."

The attack on Clark seems unfair to me as well. Noah's key points are that Clark hasn't done anything more significant than enrich herself, that recent studies suggest television viewing is not good for children, and that Baby Einstein is the leading edge of a movement that makes untrue claims to women so they can feel safe about ignoring their children.

The first point is not true. Since selling Baby Einstein in 2001, Clark created a program, called The Safe Side, whose videos instruct children about the dangers of using the Internet and talking to strangers. She persuaded *America's Most Wanted* host John Walsh to join her effort, and they donated a video to every school district in Texas. The presidential nod was for this as much as for Baby Einstein. Noah's second point—about the possible danger of showing videos to babies—is possibly true, but not relevant to Clark. The studies suggesting dangers to babies from television exposure were published only after Clark had sold Baby Einstein to Disney, and none addressed the baby video phenomenon directly. Finally, whether or not the baby video industry preys on the insecurities of new parents, ordinary parents believe that there is some good in exposing their babies to classical music and foreign languages while watching slowly moving, pleasing images. Assuming that these consumers are all chumps just because of two unduplicated medical studies doesn't seem fair either.

Even if the attack on Julie Aigner-Clark seems mean-spirited, something in the critique resonates with me. Watching Clark on television, I cannot help but have the feeling "Why her? What makes this woman so special?" She looks like an ordinary person standing up there in front of the entire nation, like just another soccer mom. But that is also her appeal. Julie Clark was never a marketer or a businessperson. She was an English teacher and then a stay-at-home mom. The evil motives assigned to her are off base. Clark wasn't trying to swindle anxious mothers—she was one. "I was a real, honest-to-God stay-at-home mother and I wanted this for my child," Clark says, "and I was lucky that other mothers felt the same way." In other words, Baby Einstein was an Accidental Brand.

The Julie Clark I meet a month after the State of the Union address in suburban Denver is an entirely different person from the one I have seen on television. The early March day is the warmest on record in Denver, the temperature already topping 75 degrees when she greets me at her door. Clark is casually dressed in sandals, torn jeans, and a David Bowie concert t-shirt. Her shoulder-length, golden hair hangs loose over angular features. She is wearing no jewelry except for a slender wedding band (no diamond) and a small gold Rolex watch that might pass for a knockoff. A pickup truck, parked in the circular driveway directly in front of the front door to her house, is splattered with mud. I'm late, having crawled along in Denver traffic to reach her, and she hustles me into the pickup because we are running late for school.

As I have met more accidental entrepreneurs, I've found that they fall into two categories. The first group, which includes Gary Erickson at Clif Bar and Gert Boyle at Columbia Sportswear, sees the business as a lifelong pursuit. These folks become so attached to their creation that they hang on through the difficult transition from running a company where everyone knows each other to masterminding a true corporation with hierarchy and lots of bright-faced people they don't recognize. The second class of entrepreneur never really wants to run a corporation at all. When the business gets to the size where being in charge means doing more administrative than creative work, these founders get out. Clark falls into the second category.

When Julie Clark sold Baby Einstein to Disney in 2001, it had exactly 8 employees responsible for the $22 million in revenue it produced that year. Julie and her husband, Bill Clark, who was COO of Baby Einstein, netted about $40 million on that sale. Even if it put them in the same league with minor investment bankers and successful law firm partners rather than the Bill Gateses or Warren Buffetts of the world, there was enough money for Clark to do whatever she wanted. So it is revealing that in the sixth year of her retirement, she has come full circle to where she started out before meeting her husband, having children, and starting Baby Einstein. Julie Clark is once again teaching English.

The private middle school where Clark teaches is a model of progressive modesty. Classes are extremely small, with 15 students on average, and from what I can tell, the level of the teaching is excellent. The physical structure of the building is decidedly modest, however. The building is a two-story affair with institutional fluorescent lighting and cinderblock walls. A recent renovation has brightened things up by adding multicolor tiles to the floor and bright yellow paint to the walls.

If there is irony in a multimillionaire and famous entrepreneur teaching poetry to sixth and seventh graders, none of the kids in Clark's class see it. They shuffle in with the ragged steps of teenagers, looking curiously at me sitting in the back of the class. One of the last students to arrive is Clark's daughter Aspen, the older child who accompanied her to the State of the Union address. Aspen is golden-skinned and confident, with an unusually upright bearing for a 12-year-old. Unlike some of her classmates, she makes direct eye contact with me when her mother introduces her.

Clark starts the class out by reading a poem. It is "Hurt Hawks" by Robinson Jeffers, about a man who kills a wounded hawk out of mercy. It could be a parable of adolescence, but the reason it delights the class is because it plays to the adolescent obsession with death:

He is strong and pain is worse to the strong, incapacity is worse
The curs of the day come and torment him
At distance, no one but death the redeemer will humble that
    head,

The intrepid readiness, the terrible eyes.
The wild God of the world is sometimes merciful to those
That ask mercy, not often to the arrogant.

What I notice first about Clark during the class is how well she listens. Any student who speaks has her full attention—her entire body is still. Like great entertainers and politicians, she completely focuses on the person in front of her. In my experience, this is a very unusual quality in an entrepreneur or a CEO. She also has a natural affinity for children. They speak to her both familiarly and respectfully, which is a difficult balance to achieve with young teens. They also joke—when a student mentions the odd name of a friend, Clark says, "It's just amazing what parents will name their children. I mean, you have them naming their kids after a tree. Wait—I actually did that." She deadpans the last bit as Aspen smiles, and it's clear that one of the main attractions of teaching for Clark is the opportunity to spend time with her daughter.

Teaching is a luxury for Julie Clark. After graduating from Michigan State University in 1988, she took a job teaching adult education in East Detroit because she couldn't get a day job teaching children. It took her two years to finally get that day job, and it was teaching English in middle school, just as she does now. After four years, the strains of supporting herself on a teacher's salary persuaded Clark to seek other employment and she found a job working for a company called Optical Data Corporation.

Optical Data was founded to bring a new technology from the 1980s (the laser disk) into the classroom. The ability to store vast amounts of visual data on a single disk gave schools in this pre-Internet era new options for teaching and helped eliminate carousels of slides. Julie was paired with a salesperson at Optical Data and her job was to show schoolteachers how to use the technology. The company was losing money and Julie was laid off after just a year, but it was a pivotal moment in her life for two reasons: First, because Julie met her husband Bill at Optical, where Bill was CEO. Second, because helping middle school teachers use laser disk technology planted the seed in Julie's mind that video could be an effective teaching tool.

After leaving Optical Data, Julie moved in with Bill and into "The Hills," a nondescript, sprawling condo complex in Bedminster, New Jersey, south of Morristown. She took a job working on child assault prevention for a nonprofit. In 1994, Julie became pregnant for the first time. She left her job after delivering Aspen and became a stay-at-home mom. A year later, Optical Data was sold to Cox and Bill moved Julie and their newborn daughter Aspen to the Atlanta area.

Even in New Jersey, Julie had begun to think about the sights and sounds that babies are exposed to every day. Julie didn't like a lot of the media influences that surround a child's life—from advertising to music videos—and wanted to give Aspen a strong foundation in the things that were important to her. This meant classical music, art, poetry and foreign languages. Clark found that some of this existed for young children, but virtually none for babies. And there were no baby videos to speak of. She was looking for something that did not exist—a way to stimulate her baby's mind with images and sounds that were important to her. She didn't have time to do anything about it while she was apart from Bill, but the idea did not leave her mind.

When Clark moved to Georgia, she and Bill bought a house in Alpharetta, "otherwise known as purgatory," in Julie's words. As Aspen passed her first birthday and Julie was able to sleep through the night, her thoughts turned back to the idea of a learning video for a baby. She decided to make a video. I ask Clark what made her take this step, the step that so few people with good ideas take. "I'd seen Bill do it at Optical Data, so I wasn't intimidated. At first, I treated it like a hobby. That took a lot of pressure off."

Julie was lucky that she had a friend who owned video equipment and let her borrow it for an entire year. She also had a mostly empty basement that became her office and production studio. A black velvet drop cloth was the entire "set" for the video. Since coming up with the idea for a baby video when Aspen was born, Julie had carefully watched what her daughter was attracted to. She noticed that slow movement, such as that of a diorama, was endlessly fascinating to Aspen. She also saw that certain colors and objects were more compelling than others. Clark didn't convene a focus group of mothers or conduct research to see what she should put in the video—she just put in what she knew her own daughter liked. She also had another motive for completing the video; midway through production, she became pregnant again. In all, it took her a year to complete the first Baby Einstein video and cost Clark and her husband $17,000 in personal savings.

Personal experience

The first video is called *Baby Einstein Language Nursery.* Julie provides the narrative voice, as she did in all the videos produced while she owned the company. The video is incredibly simple. The background is black. It starts with the music from "Pop Goes the Weasel" playing as Julie's manicured hand pushes the button to a simple popup toy—which pops up. Julie says, "Hello." Then the Baby Einstein logo and the words "Language Nursery" slowly draw themselves on the screen. Next we see a fish tank—a straight-on image that looks real enough to send a Siamese into conniptions. Then a second woman's voice, speaking in German, reads a poem while different shapes appear slowly, one after another, on the screen. For an adult watching without the presence of a lovable tyke, the video is enough to induce restless leg syndrome. It is like *Blue's Clues* in this sense—what seem like painfully slow, disconnected images to us can hold endless fascination for babies.

Or so parents tell me when I ask them about Baby Einstein. "Our son loved them," one tells me. "As soon as we'd switch it on, he'd just stare at them for 25 minutes. It was really helpful because he never drank enough formula, but he would drink more when he was watching the videos." What is so fascinating about this video to me is the way in which it subverts adult expectations. Instead of being presented with a narrative flow, characters, and action, we see still images and set pieces with a mostly unrelated soundtrack. In other words, Baby Einstein is the video version of a storyboard book. It works more or less the same way that a baby book does—giving the baby stimulus and allowing the parent to point and narrate. The idea is simple, but powerful. It is also very different from anything that existed before, including standouts for slightly older children such as *Sesame Street* and *Blue's Clues*. This is another reason that the criticism of Baby Einstein and the genre seems a bit off target. Studies warn against letting young children watch television in general, but none have tried measuring the particular effects of baby videos, still a new genre. Baby Einstein moves a lot slower than other children's television, really no faster than the pages of a book turning.

Just as with John Peterman's venture into catalog retailing, Julie Clark was gifted with a complete lack of knowledge about the "rules" of video. *Baby Einstein Language Nursery* breaks them all. It doesn't have a catchy theme song, doesn't feature high production quality, doesn't even use sets or always keep the pictures and soundtrack in synch. Above all, it doesn't move quickly to keep children entertained and it doesn't try to appeal to adults. One nice element is the presence of Clark and her children. "There's a certain quality to them," one parent tells me, "and we've seen quite a few other videos. Part of it is that you can see Julie Clark and her kids. The youngest one is a baby in the earliest videos. Then you see her get older. It's almost like watching them grow up."

Clark enjoyed making the Baby Einstein Language Nursery video, but selling it was a nightmare. "I had literally never sold a product in my life," she says, "and I didn't get a lot of support outside my own house. When I would go to a playgroup and tell other women, they didn't jump all over it and say, 'What a great idea!' They were like, 'Well . . . . okay.'" Still, she persisted, driven by her strong belief that the video would be good for babies. Clark sent copies of the video to Toys "R" Us and other big retailers she located online, but she never heard a word from any of them. She also sent the Baby Einstein Language Nursery video to a variety of magazines. Here she had more luck. *Parenting* magazine wrote a positive review of the video. Suddenly, Julie Clark found herself in business.

Running a business meant dealing with issues Clark had not considered before. "I realized that I had to accept credit card payments. How do you do that? Getting the tapes duplicated and having boxes made and shrink-wrapped wasn't hard, but what about shipping? It wasn't a lot of volume but suddenly I was the order entry person, warehouse manager and mailroom clerk at the same time."

Clark was initially selling the videos direct to consumers, operating from her basement. The garage became her warehouse. Still, Clark kept looking for retail distribution for the Baby Einstein video. A friend told her that she should go to a trade show—something Julie did not even realize existed. The industry show for children's videos is called Toy Fair and takes place every year at the Jacob K. Javits Convention Center in New York City. Clark could barely scrape together the money for the Toy Fair entry pass from her meager earnings, so there was no question of exhibiting.

→ Trade show

The Javits Center is an awkward, unlovely structure on the West Side of Manhattan, near the Hudson River. It is laid out like three large shoeboxes with holes cut in the sides, linking them. The convention space incorporates 10 separate exhibition halls on two levels, with over 300,000 square feet of floor space. Although small by modern standards and unable to host massive events like the Consumer Electronics Show (held annually in Las Vegas), Javits can still be confusing and intimidating for first-timers. Visitors may enter the Javits Center through one of a series of glass doors on different levels for their show only to realize that they're a good quarter mile from their show. ToyFair had over 20,000 attendees, and Julie felt completely overwhelmed by the hubbub in the main exhibition hall. But she had a mission. She had identified a small, upscale retailer called The Right Start as the best possible place to carry her video. She spent two days wandering the halls and looking at name badges, trying to find someone from The Right Start, until she literally ran into a group of eight women from the retailer.

"They must have thought I was crazy, but I was able to convince one of the women, named Wendy, to take a look at the video. That's all I got—her first name. I didn't hear anything for two and a half weeks, so I finally called their headquarters and asked to speak to Wendy. The receptionist told me that she had left the company and gave me the name of the woman replacing her. When I got through to her I told a white lie—that Wendy had loved the videos and was going to pass it on to her to look at. This woman paused for a moment and I could hear her shuffling things around. They she said, 'Okay, I see the video on the desk here, but I don't have a note from her or anything.' But she agreed to take a look at it." The new buyer called Clark back the next day with an order for 60 videos. All 60 sold out in a single day and The Right Start reordered. Then they asked for another title in six months. And this is where fate intervened for Baby Einstein.

The second video Clark produced was called *Baby Mozart*. She had toyed with calling it "Baby Einstein: Mozart" or some other combination of words, but in the end decided that simpler was better. This video hit store shelves in February 1998, and just two weeks later, a scientific study was released that appeared to prove that listening to Mozart could improve brain functions in babies. The story quickly reached the national headlines. They called it "the Mozart Effect." Baby Einstein exploded, with sales jumping from $100,000 in 1997 to $1,000,000 in 1998.

As we leave Clark's middle school, I get a clear look at the Rockies. They're omnipresent on a sunny day in Denver, hovering over the background like a pipe organ in a church. The snow-capped peaks look unreal to my New Yorker eye. It's more like a painted backdrop on the set of a colorized Hollywood movie. And it seems out of place against a backdrop of Best Buys and Bed, Bath & Beyonds. We pull into a shopping mall where we are meeting Julie's husband, Bill, and their longtime collaborator, Jeff Mettais, for lunch. The restaurant is P.F. Chang's. It is one of these new, upscale casual-dining behemoths that seem to have sprung up everywhere in the past few years. We walk in and are greeted by a terminally perky hostess. The interior of the restaurant looks to me like a ski lodge that has been decorated by Pottery Barn.

Bill is older than Julie by nearly 13 years and he complements her personality. Where Julie is energetic, impulsive, and demanding, Bill is calm, measured, and flexible. One of Bill's biggest roles was as a professional mentor for Julie. Even before he joined Baby Einstein, Bill was an entrepreneurial role model for her. The company he was running when the pair met, Optical Data, was partially funded by

ABC. The concept of using laser disks to bring vast amounts of information and images to the classroom seemed revolutionary when it launched. Unfortunately, it blossomed just in time to be outmoded by the DVD and then the Internet. When I ask Bill about the company, he smiles. "We made a lot of history and lost a lot of money."

Baby Einstein was clearly something different. Just as the first video was nearing completion, Julie and Bill moved from Alpharetta to Denver. Bill took a job with a nonprofit specializing in the needs of entrepreneurs in the Denver area. A year later he left when it became painfully evident that Baby Einstein was growing faster than Julie could handle on her own. The division of labor at Baby Einstein was straightforward. Bill took over operations and began to put together a strategic plan for the company. He helped Julie think through the intellectual property issues for Baby Einstein and was able to secure strong trademark protection for the company's branded products. He also helped think through the life cycle of the consumer and was instrumental in getting Julie to launch a line of videos for children 1 to 3 years old to complement the offerings for newborns. Julie was CEO and had complete control over the videos (and later, books), the brand, and the creative process. "Baby Einstein videos and books were really handcrafted products with Julie's fingerprints all over every single one," Bill says, as he sips at a bowl of soup.

It is this intimacy, this handcrafted authenticity, which gave the Baby Einstein brand its extraordinary strength. As with most of the other brands in this book, the success of Baby Einstein hinged on Julie Clark's ability to persuasively tell her own story—that of a stay-at-home mother who created a product that she wanted for her own baby. This "by us, for us" mentality, along with a strong story, is what sets Accidental Brands apart from corporate brands. Nobody likes buying things from nameless, faceless corporations. A brand gives a company a face. An Accidental Brand has a clearer face and a stronger story. Whether it was during her appearance on *Oprah* or the back cover of a Baby Einstein book, Julie Clark knew how to tell her own story.

Accidental Brands tend to be very careful about hiring. A bad hiring decision can pollute the corporate DNA and bring down the morale of the entire organization. Thus, most companies who experience the kind of explosive growth Baby Einstein enjoyed between 1998 and 2000 (which increased tenfold as sales went from $1,000,000 to $10,000,000) hire in proportion to their sales. Not so with Baby Einstein. In total, the Baby Einstein Company had just eight employees in 2001 when it was sold to Disney. Sales results for that last year were $22 million—a staggering $2.75 million in revenue per employee. I asked Bill Clark at lunch about the small size of the company and he characterized it as a lifestyle choice. Managing a huge group of employees changes the nature of the workload for the CEO and COO. Hiring any faster would have ruined family life for both Bill and Julie. And they really considered employee members to be family as well. Of the eight employees in Baby Einstein at the time of the sale in 2001, seven are working on one of the Clarks' two new ventures, namely The Safe Side and Memory Lane.

In 1999, Disney Publishing approached Julie and asked her to license a series of books under the Baby Einstein trademark. Clark was intrigued because she had always wanted to write and thought that books were a natural complement to the Baby Einstein videos. She agreed, with the caveat that she be given complete creative control, and began to produce a series of books that numbered 20 by the time of the company sale, contributing significantly to Baby Einstein revenues.

By 2000, Baby Einstein had attracted a great deal of competition, and both Bill and Julie felt that the company needed additional capital in order to stay on top of the industry it had spawned. Their workdays were getting longer and longer, making it harder to have a normal family life, and the company was testing their personal values. Baby Einstein was producing video, Julie was creating books for Disney to sell and produce on a licensed basis, and Clark had also introduced a Little Einstein line for small children. The complexity of the growing operation was enormous, and it was clear that major investment was needed to take it to the next level. Faced with a fundamental life decision, the Clarks agreed quickly on what to do. They elected to sell the business. It was a simple decision, Bill says. "This thing's going to eat our lives up, and we just asked ourselves, 'What's more important, our kids or our business?' "

Julie nods emphatically. "We never ran a single ad and we never did any marketing. Baby Einstein was all word of mouth. We knew that we would have to sell it eventually because we wanted to spend as much time as we could with our kids. The surprise—what we never anticipated—was that we would have this tremendous success with the business."

So Julie and Bill called Disney. The couple's experience with Disney Books had been positive and they liked the fit between the two brands. Julie says she told Disney, in effect, "We like you and we're calling you first. We're selling the business and we want to know if you are interested." They were interested. Ten months later, Julie and Bill Clark sold Baby Einstein to Disney for $40 million.

Of the entrepreneurs profiled in this book, only two—Clark and Roxanne Quimby—have sold their businesses outright. For both, the loss of control seems to have been like watching a child go to college. Buying a brand from the founder is a delicate business and Disney was clear about the endgame. At one point during negotiations with the lawyers, Disney's point man put his hand on Julie's and looked at her sharply, saying, "You understand we're buying the right to run this business the way we want to, right?"

Julie understood—and didn't. When the sale was completed and Julie had the customary title of "retained consultant," she expected to hold on to creative control over the product. Instead, she was gradually pushed aside. Then she reached a breaking point. "I thought it was really going to be great to work with Disney, but then it wasn't. So I finally said, 'That's that and it's done, and I'm really proud because this would never have existed without me.'"

Disney even brought in another mother to run the business—but this one had an MBA. "She said something like, 'We're going to make this thing slick,' and I knew it was trouble right then," Bill says. After some further frustrations, Julie says, "In the end it became impossible for me to work with Disney. I couldn't let go and it didn't work out." → *they pushed her out*

On the revenue side, Disney has done a remarkable job growing the brand. By 2006, in just four short years after the acquisition, Baby Einstein revenue grew nearly tenfold, to over $200 million. And Disney has resisted the impulse to "Disneyfy" the brand. The same logo Julie drew at her dining room table in Alpharetta, Georgia in 1996 is still the one on Baby Einstein books and videos; the Disney logo, while there, is small and subdued. But in another sense, Bill's comments about the Disney attitude to the brand ring true. Professional actors have replaced the Clark family (Aspen and Sierra used to be regulars) in newer Baby Einstein videos, and the videos' look and feel is no longer handmade. In addition, much of the revenue for the Baby Einstein brand now comes from licensed toys, baby toiletries, baby gear, and party supplies, among other items. In short, the Baby Einstein brand is not as authentic as it was under Clark. It is no longer the loving result of one mother's efforts for other mothers.

As we leave lunch, I ask Clark when she realized that she had actually become successful—that she had made it. She laughs, and points to a DSW store in the mall we're driving out of. "It was right there, actually. I can literally remember being at that store and having two pairs of shoes in my hands, trying to decide which pair to buy and then thinking, 'Wow, now I can buy them both.'" It says something about the intimacy of Clark's dreams that everything she values in life—from her children to the first (and last) corporate offices of Baby Einstein to the people who help her build that company—can be found within an arm's reach in her original neighborhood of Denver.

involved community

I am curious about Bill's comment about "Julie's fingerprints" being all over every one of the products of Baby Einstein. The phrase suggests an obsession with detail that I haven't yet seen from Clark. Unrelenting attention to the small things is common among Accidental Brand entrepreneurs, but Julie seems far too relaxed to be obsessive. As we drive to the home studio of Mark Burr, who edited all of the Baby Einstein videos for Clark during the independent run of the company, Clark almost has to divert to a Wal-Mart to buy a Baby Einstein video, as she is temporarily without a copy, but Mark has one. Burr lives in an unremarkable townhouse development a few minutes' drive from Clark's old neighborhood, where he has turned the first floor into a full video production studio, with a converted bedroom featuring a full AVID video editor.

Julie is working on a speech she will be giving to Microsoft a week later and it quickly becomes clear that she has something very specific in mind. To an outsider, the process of video editing is tedious, but Clark is plainly no outsider. She relishes the chance to paste the perfect story together with video bits from the Baby Einstein and Safe Side tapes. She also seems to have an encyclopedic knowledge of her own work. When Mark is looking for footage to fill out the music from an edited line, she knows exactly the single scene from among a dozen videos to pull. They talk by shorthand, completing each other's sentences and thoughts. I later ask Clark about the Microsoft talk and she says, "I loved it because I was standing in front of this roomful of Harvard MBAs and really, really brilliant people and sharing my story. And I realized they were actually learning something from me."

The video-editing session reinforces my feeling that Baby Einstein was a labor of love for Clark (and it also reinforces my growing conviction that I will never direct feature films). And perhaps that is the secret of the brand. For Julie Clark, Baby Einstein was a child no less than Aspen or Sierra. Julie's entire focus is family, and it has been consistently so for her entire adult life. As long as Baby Einstein was part of the family and brought the family together, Clark handled it brilliantly. When the business threatened the balance and sanity of her family, she gave it up. When Disney took control of Baby Einstein, Clark could no longer contribute. She couldn't be a foster parent to her own child. FAM FIRST mentality

Mark chuckles when I ask him if Clark is obsessive. "Well, Julie is unusual because she is not only creative but very detail oriented. She knows exactly what she wants." Julie smiles, and reminds Mark that he had once—after margaritas apparently—told Clark that she was difficult to work with. Mark shakes his head and changes the subject. He won't be baited. But it is easy to see that Burr has worked so well with Clark because he knew how to surrender ownership to her and focus on becoming intuitive at knowing what she might want.

Letting go was difficult. By the end of 2002, Julie Clark was completely done with Baby Einstein—she was no longer consulting for Disney. So she channeled her effort into a new endeavor. This one came from a new anxiety she had acquired as the mother of two girls. She was not confident that they were getting the right instruction in school on how to protect themselves from strangers and the pitfalls found on the Internet. In 2003, she founded a company called The Safe Side to address the dangers of childhood. She decided to use the familiar tool of instructional videos in a new way to show kids good practices with strangers and with people who were not strangers but might still pose a danger.

This time around, Julie's celebrity from her Baby Einstein success gave her a leg up. She had capital and a great deal of support. In late 2002, Clark was asked to appear on *The John Walsh Show*. This was the same John Walsh who hosts *America's Most Wanted*, and Clark saw an opportunity. She said she'd appear on the talk show only if she got an hour of Walsh's time to tell him about The Safe Side. The gambit worked and Clark got Walsh to sign on with her to support The Safe Side. Clark spent an entire year shooting the first Safe Side video, investing $400,000 of her own money to produce it—a hefty step up from the $17,000 the first Baby Einstein video had cost her. In January 2004, the video was ready for editing. Then, a few days into the editing process, disaster struck.

"I had worked out the night before and lifted and I was sore. I was sitting in the editing studio, rubbing under my arm and I felt this tiny, tiny bump. I didn't think about it for a couple of days and then I decided to try to find the spot again. It took awhile but I finally found it. Then I took a permanent marker and put a dot on the spot."

Clark went to see her doctor, who was conscientious enough to send her for more testing. The next few days were a whirlwind. "On Wednesday morning, I had a mammogram. They looked at the films and sent me back to my doctor. I knew that wasn't good. I had a biopsy on Thursday, and by Friday I was diagnosed with a carcinoma, an invasive cancer."

I ask Clark about her reaction to the diagnosis as we sit outside her new house, overlooking her pool and the mountains. She peers into the distance as she answers me. "Your whole life kind of goes black and all you think about is your kids—they were 9 and 7. I had them spend the night at my best friend's house. On Saturday, they came home and we sat them down at the kitchen table and I told them, 'Mommy got some bad news. I have cancer, but I don't have the kind you die from.' That's what I told them, because I needed to tell them something but I didn't want to terrify them." Over the next several days, Clark did what most people do these days when they learn they have cancer: she used the Internet to read everything she could find about the disease. And she came to a firm resolution.

"I decided that I wanted to get it out and never have it happen again. I decided to have a double mastectomy, which was a radical choice. I saw five oncologists that first week and none of them recommended a double mastectomy. All of them said chemo, a lumpectomy, and radiation. But the thing is, all of these oncologists put you in a group. They have a standard path that they follow with all breast cancer patients. But my cancer was my own, it was unique. I didn't want it coming back. Ten days after the cancer was diagnosed, I had a double mastectomy. I had no chemo and no radiation." Here, she sighs and allows herself a smile. "I had my three-year anniversary on Saturday—three years with no signs of recurrence. That's a big deal."

After recovering from the surgery, Julie's first reaction to the cancer was to plunge back into work. She returned to The Safe Side with a vengeance and shifted her strategy away from retail sales towards schools. With Bill's help, Julie championed an effort to donate a free video to every school district in the state of Texas, which is what got her noticed by one of President Bush's West Wing staffers. She continued working at a blistering pace for almost three years, until everything caught up with her.

By 2006, Julie and Bill had left their first Denver neighborhood, and the basement that had seen Baby Einstein exceed $5 million in revenue, and moved to a dream house further out in the Denver suburbs. The stunning, 10,000-square-foot contemporary sits on a hill overlooking Denver with a clear view of the Rockies. As we walk through the house I get a sense of the vast scale that money buys in the suburbs these days. The ceilings are 25 feet high and it looks like it might take scaffolding to change a light bulb. Downstairs, Bill has put in a home theater that seats 10 in front of a 75-inch, high-definition TV, just past the requisite pool table and around the corner from his office. The kitchen is modern and marble and there is a full dining table outdoors as well as the one indoors. The backyard pool is landscaped with stone and sits next to a cushioned basketball court. Julie's office is on the main floor and looks airy—and slightly uncomfortable. In fact, the whole house seems a bit intimidating, somewhat larger than life. The feeling I get from Julie is of the slightest bit of buyer's remorse. "It's a lot of house—sometimes we wonder if we need it," she says as I crane my head up to see some of the mementos from the early days of Baby Einstein.

Finally, in 2006, Clark began to change gears. "I decided 'I just don't want to work this hard.' The cancer was a big wake-up call; it just took some time to get the message. I thought, 'You've been given this wonderful gift. You had this super-successful business; you've got more money than you ever thought you'd have in your life. You were a teacher, for God's sake!'" She pauses and laughs. "I mean, I was making $25,000 a year. My kids are still young enough that they like me and I can enjoy them. I was ready to just shelve The Safe Side, but Bill and I had talked a lot about the school opportunities, and he decided to jump in and take it over. I decided to go back to teaching."

So in the fall of 2006, after a hiatus of nearly 15 years, Julie returned to teaching, and in the same private middle school where her daughter was in sixth grade. She came back to teach poetry and English and to spend more time with her children. She is also training to teach a humane education program—geared to teach children how to care for animals, around the Denver School system. If she has any regrets, they are impossible to detect. As the light begins to drain out of the Colorado sky, I sense that Julie Clark is finally exactly where she wants to be.

THE ANARCHIST: ROXANNE QUIMBY (BURT'S BEES)

> What is most striking in the Maine wilderness is the continuousness of the forest, with fewer open intervals or glades than you had imagined. . . . It is even more grim and wild than you had anticipated, a damp and intricate wilderness, in the spring everywhere wet and miry.
>
> The aspect of the country indeed is universally stern and savage . . . .
>
> What a place to live, what a place to die and be buried in!
>
> —Henry David Thoreau, *The Maine Woods*, "Ktaadn"

Modern-day Maine mediates an uneasy truce between its rugged past—the Maine of loggers and trappers—and its current status as favored getaway for the rich. The jetway at Portland International Jetport straddles the line with a banner that reads "Welcome Home" and features line drawings of a moose on one side and a lobster on the other. As I'm neither tourist nor lobsterman, I walk quickly through the small terminal building and outside. It's a cold spring day and the weather is foreboding. Storm clouds swirl overhead, leaving the lush greenery of Portland under a gray light.

After a few moments, my ride appears. A fifty-something woman bounces out of a navy blue Volvo station wagon with a handwritten "For Sale" sign in the window. She is tall and sports long braided ponytails. "Hello, David!" she says as she extends her hand. Then she starts talking at a rapid clip while I scramble to keep up. My first thought is that it's Heidi, only with a 160 IQ. Instead, it's Roxanne Quimby, founder of Burt's Bees.

I have been looking forward to meeting Quimby for a long time. Several years earlier, a student of mine at NYU had written a paper on Burt's Bees for a class project on entrepreneurs who created large brands without formal marketing training. This student's best friend attended college with Quimby's daughter. The student wove a heroic tale of this woman who started with absolutely nothing and built an empire off the humble bee. When I first tried to contact Quimby, she was in Paris taking a pastry class at Le Cordon Bleu, having sold Burt's Bees for $175 million, and I had little luck reaching her. Fortunately, I was able to contact her a year later, and now I find myself in the seat next to her as we weave through light traffic in Portland.

Quimby drives me through the downtown area of Portland to the house where she's currently staying. She owns a summer place in Winter Harbor, four houses in Portland, and four more down in Palm Beach, Florida. "I don't really know where I live right now," she confesses as we pull in front of a pretty, two-story brick house in a tree-lined and historic part of Portland's West End. In her life after Burt's Bees, real estate has become a hobby and passion for Quimby. She buys homes, restores them, and then sells them at a profit. "I'm just camping in this house while I supervise the restoration," she tells me, and she's right. As she shows me around the house, I see nice details like inlaid wood, lots of half-finished paintwork, but almost no personal possession beyond a laptop computer. Roxanne travels light.

This particular house has special meaning to Quimby, because it belonged to the father of one of her personal heroes, former Governor Percival Baxter. Baxter served in Maine's Senate and its House of Representatives before becoming governor in 1921. He had a great passion for the wilderness and fought unsuccessfully to preserve the area around Maine's highest peak, Mount Katahdin, as both a legislator and governor. The Great Northern Paper Company owned most of the land around Katahdin at the time, and after the stock market crash of 1929 the company agreed to sell Baxter 6,000 acres around the mountain for $25,000. He deeded the acres to the state on the condition that the park "shall forever be used for public park and recreational purposes, shall be forever left in the natural wild state, shall forever be kept as a sanctuary for wild beasts and birds, that no road or ways for motor vehicles shall hereafter ever be constructed thereon or therein." Baxter continued to add to the park until his death at the age of 92 in 1969, and the park now covers almost 210,000 acres. He used his legislative experience to place the park under control of an independent authority, thus ensuring that the state of Maine cannot easily change the land's use. Baxter, as you might expect, is a legend in Maine.

Quimby is fast on her way to matching Baxter's feat, in a far more difficult era. After selling Burt's Bee's in 2003, she took over half of the cash portion of the sale, some $85 million, and put it into a trust. Her goal is to extend Baxter State Park to the Penobscot River to the east, as Governor Baxter had originally intended. In the process, she wants to double the size of the park by protecting an additional 200,000 acres. As a conservationist, Quimby may be more impressive than

Baxter because, in the course of just four years, she has succeeded in purchasing and protecting over 85,000 acres. And she has done this in spite of a far more complicated legal and regulatory environment and opposition from logging interests, hunting, and ATV groups who stand to lose access to the land.

Yet all of this has not been enough to keep Quimby fully occupied. In addition to renovating houses and protecting the Maine wilderness, she started an Internet café in Winter Harbor and had planned to open a cooking school there. She is also founder of The Happy Green Bee, a company in North Carolina that sells organic cotton clothing for children. For good measure, Roxanne has started the Quimby Family Foundation, which gives $600,000 a year to Maine nonprofits. Maintaining these separate activities necessitates constantly shuttling among Portland, Winter Harbor, Raleigh, and Palm Beach. It's no wonder that Quimby feels like she's still camping out. And it's appropriate. Because Roxanne's great fortune, both literally and figuratively, started in the Maine woods some 23 years ago—with a few bees.

Roxanne Quimby is the daughter of an engineer. She was born in Cambridge, Massachusetts, but moved frequently throughout New England during her childhood, finally landing a few miles away in Lexington, Massachusetts, for high school. Quimby had an interest in art and went to California for college, attending the San Francisco Art Institute. Roxanne arrived in California at the peak of the hippie movement, and it profoundly influenced her. "I took a vow of poverty," she says as we sip tea in the living room of the Baxter house, "How did that work out for you?" I ask, looking around, and she laughs: "Not the way I had expected!"

After college, Roxanne headed back east with her boyfriend, George. The two had decided to live simply and they became part of the "back to the land" movement of the 1970s. "We had checked out land in northern California, Oregon, and Washington and it was still too expensive. We came all the way across the country because we knew it was going to be one coast or the other. We went to Vermont . . . the real estate guy there said, 'You gotta go to Maine if you only have $3,000.' He was right: land was $100 an acre. We bought 30 acres and built a little cabin on it in Guilford, about 50 miles north of Bangor."

I ask Roxanne why she chose that life and she says, "I was sure that we were all doomed, and I was doing my best to figure out how to survive. It was a transformative experience because my family had been residents of suburban America, and that's where I was raised. It put me in touch with nature in a way that I had never had been before, because everything was outdoors."

The cabin that Roxanne and George built was off the grid. It had no electricity and no running water. I ask Roxanne what that was like and she says, "Our fuel was out in the woodshed, our food was in our root cellar or in the garden, and our water was in the spring. We had to go out many times a day, and when we were building the cabin, we lived outdoors. Maine really doesn't let you forget you're outdoors. It's always cold or windy or rainy or sunny or buggy. I had a rutabaga three times a day because that's all that would grow up there."

Roxanne and George married, and they had twins. That made living off the grid even harder. "I developed a real sensitivity to daylight, nighttime, where my water came from, where my food came from, how hard it is to heat a house if you are relying on cutting your own wood with a crosscut saw and an axe, and hauling it in. I became, because of the circumstances, very conservative. Once you haul a five-gallon bucket of water for a quarter of a mile, you don't just slop it around. You wash your baby in it, and then you wash the floor with it. There's this descending order of uses. You really think about things that way, or else you are going to spend a lot of time hauling water."

The combination of sturdy practicality and childish enthusiasm is something I have not encountered before; at least not to the extent I see it in Roxanne. Living at the mercy of nature toughened her without hardening her. The experience deepened her sense of being connected to the environment and heightened her awareness of our dependence on it.

If Quimby's experience living off the grid was successful, her marriage was not. In her mid-30s, she found herself single with two children. When she divorced George, they sold the cabin. She ended up living with the children in a tent by a lake. Two tents, actually, one for sleeping and another for living. One day, Roxanne recalls, a thunderstorm came whipping in from the lake, "It was so violent I was really afraid, so we got out of the tents and ran to my car, an old Rambler. Then the tents blew into the lake. It was amazing that the kids just thought it was an adventure."

She started to have doubts. Her children were socializing with kids from households with electricity and running water. "They were wearing Goodwill clothes and I didn't want them to be made fun of. They already had this terrible onus of not knowing the TV shows that children watch." Roxanne had taken a vow of poverty for herself, but she was increasingly uncomfortable imposing it on her children. She began to cast around for a way to make money.

In the spring of 1984, Roxanne's opportunity arrived by chance. She was hitchhiking to the post office and Burt Shavitz stopped to give her a ride. She recognized Burt, a man she'd seen but had never talked to. "Burt sold honey on the side of the road. I'd seen the stand before. He used to be there on the weekends. He fascinated me because he was such a freak—I am very attracted to the oddballs of the world." The ride was short and the pair didn't speak much, but the door had been opened. Quimby was working part-time as a waitress at a local motor lodge in Dexter, and Burt began chatting with her when he stopped by. Eventually, Roxanne asked Burt if she could help him out over the summer so she could learn how to keep bees. Burt isn't one to turn down free help, and he agreed.

Roxanne piles me back into the station wagon to drive downtown for lunch. The car is not actually hers but her daughter's. The daughter wants to sell the car, and Roxanne has volunteered to drive it around for the mobile advertising effect while she is out of town. Quimby picks a trendy little restaurant called Walter's on Exchange Street, in the middle of the old port. As we walk in to sit down, I realize that I ate in this same place several years before, on my last visit to Portland, when I came to see a friend who was teaching at Bowdoin College. The décor is nicer this time, but the place is otherwise unchanged. I order a bowl of soup and Roxanne picks a salad.

Burt Shavitz is 14 years older than Quimby and when they met he had a very simple business model. He would get empty used one-gallon pickle jars from the local deli, fill them with honey from his bees, and sell them at a roadside stand. This netted him a few thousand dollars a year, which was enough to pay for his land taxes and the registration fee on his pickup truck. Burt was a loner, a thin man sporting a wild white beard, living in a tiny cabin with a potbellied stove. He liked puttering around his property. Beekeeping was an easy way to maintain this simple lifestyle.

Quimby was fascinated by bees. "I loved them," she says. "I really loved keeping bees. It was this whole world with a great model for productivity and cooperation. I was fascinated by those bees." Roxanne immediately saw possibilities for Burt, both professional and romantic. "I think I had this illusion that I was just what he needed, that I was going to *just* tweak him a little bit." While Roxanne did not succeed in changing Burt, their relationship lasted for over a decade and she had an immediate impact on his business. The fall came, the bees wintered, and Burt and Roxanne found that they had 3,000 pounds of honey and several hundred pounds of beeswax to sell. "Christmas was coming and I saw an opportunity to sell the honey as a giftable item, as opposed to the way Burt was selling it as a food thing." She started out by putting the honey into smaller jars, increasing the price, and decorating the jars. (Later, when I talk to Burt, he jokes, "Her plan was to sell it by the spoonful.") Burt suggested that Roxanne could make candles with the beeswax, and Roxanne got a book and soon started hand-dipping candles. With the nicely packaged honey and beeswax candles, Roxanne was ready to try her luck at a craft fair. "The first one was at the junior high school in the middle of town, and I made $200 that day selling honey and candles. It was in December of '84. I was so psyched, I just couldn't believe it. I thought, 'This is it, I'm in the money!'"

For the next five years, Roxanne and Burt sold honey and beeswax candles at craft fairs all over the state. After a few years, volumes grew and Burt had to stop keeping bees because it was more economical to buy the honey and beeswax from other beekeepers. At the same time, Quimby started experimenting with other products. "I was reading beekeeping journals from the 1800s and looking up recipes. There was a recipe for shoe polish. It was leather dressing that had beeswax in it, so I made some of that, canned it up, and put a label on it." Quimby also formulated stove polish, seamstress wax, and several other items. She was working hard to find complementary products to even out the seasonality of hand-dipped candles, 75 percent of which sell in the last quarter of the year. One of the products Quimby tried was lip balm. "It's the same thing as furniture polish," she says as I raise an eyebrow. "It just has peppermint in it instead of lavender."

Lip balm was the product that really made Burt's Bees. Quimby fiddled with the lip balm formula, adding sweet almond oil and Vitamin E into it. Instead of selling it in tubes, she used tins, round tins like the ones she used for furniture polish. The first time she took the lip balm to a craft fair, Roxanne knew she had a hit. And this is one of the lessons of business from Burt's Bees: "You have to be really open-minded about what business you are in. You might not know what business you are in for a while. Your customers will pretty much define that for you, if you're open to their suggestions." In 1986, Roxanne and Burt got a trailer to run the business from. It was parked on a piece of land Roxanne owned where they both had small cabins. Burt still lives in his.

Until 1988, it was just Quimby and Shavitz loading up his pickup with products and driving them to different craft fairs, often sleeping in the back of the pickup. In that year, Quimby hired the first employee. After 1989, when the lip balm appeared, Roxanne was hiring more people, opening an office, and starting a catalog. The office had grown to three trailers, and Quimby and Shavitz moved the business into an old bowling alley, a 150-year-old building that had started life as a general store in the nineteenth century. It was an appropriate setting for Burt's Bees, which was producing a wide array of products. Quimby created a catalog for the business in 1990. It featured everything from foot powder to dog bones. The catalog also told a bit of Burt's story, carefully redacted to highlight his charming quirkiness. With each catalog, Roxanne would write a little more of the story, so the catalogs became popular among the brand's growing tribe of devotees.

Accidental brands often grow so slowly that they give their founders the time to learn important lessons about their customers. I ask Roxanne what she learned about consumers in those years, and she has some interesting observations. "One thing that I saw is that no matter how beautiful a candle was, they would always pick it up and turn it upside down and look at the bottom of it. I thought, 'Why do they do that? There's nothing on the bottom.' The bottom is a flat surface for it to sit on. Why do they do that? They're looking for something that's hidden. It was the only part that was hidden, the bottom. I guess they wanted to look to see what's hidden.... I remember going back to my manufacturing ladies and making sure that the bottoms were finished off nicely." At the time, Quimby thought she was learning something about selling candles, but she later realized she was learning something about human desire.

"When I started selling stuff that smelled, like hand salves or lip balms, they would always smell it before they would put it on their hand. They would open the jar, my little tester. No one would ever take a dab and put it on their skin; they would always bring it to their nose and smell it, and then put it on their skin and smell it again on their skin. I realized smell is really important. I really worked with the fragrance issue a lot. It was almost as important as the packaging, because I learned that your olfactory perceptions are very primitive and deeply embedded in the mind and the brain, I think the hypothalamus. It's a very primitive old piece of the brain that recognizes smell, and it's almost undeniable, you can't intellectualize it. Something smells horrible and it's like, 'Ugh!'"

As Roxanne became more interested in fragrance, Burt's Bees was slowly transformed into a personal-care products company. She learned to formulate fragrances, and this led her into the world of essential oils. Essential oils are concentrated liquids that contain the volatile aroma compounds from plants. Each essential oil contains the distinctive scent of the plant it is derived from, and these oils are generally extracted by distillation through water or by cold pressing.

Flowers have a low volume of volatile scent oils, and these are harder to extract because they are also more sensitive to heat and often cannot be distilled with steam. For this reason, many high-volume manufacturers use industrial solvents like hexane to extract the scent of these flowers. Quimby became concerned about the petrochemical residue left in the final product. As she became more expert in formulation, she used only essential oils that had been extracted with alcohol (which can be completely removed from the oil) or CO_2 extraction under pressure, which also leaves no residue. Quimby became convinced that scent was a powerful trigger for action. "Personal care products smell and have a fragrance, and that fragrance tells a story. I wanted it to be the right story. The brain chemistry is altered through the inhalation of these petroleum products in a different way than the way an essential oil is squeezed out of flowers and has a living story to tell to a living being who can perceive it. A lot of this is totally unconscious. People really can't find the words to describe this until they're like 'Oh!' and they want more, and you watch their behavior change."

By 1991 there were 25 employees working in the old general store in Guilford, a few miles away from Roxanne's cabin in Parkman. Quimby was working madly, masterminding operations, formulating products, tweaking packaging, and trying not to be overwhelmed by accounting. "She would get up at 4:00 A.M. to go to work and not come home until 1:00 A.M. some days," says Burt, who was not interested in living the same life. As Burt's Bees became a corporation, his interest waned, although he still helped out with specific tasks. Roxanne found manufacturing and quality control especially challenging. As a woman, she was always confronting situations where men would try to tell her things worked a certain way. When they didn't work at all, she would have to learn how they actually functioned, only to learn that it was different from what she had been told.

"There were always little places where one thing was a little behind, which would keep the business stalled while we fixed it, like IT or manufacturing or accounting, or wherever it was. That would allow us to get some growth. There was never a problem with sales. That was because we never were able to meet the demand entirely, because manufacturing was always a problem. If it wasn't manufacturing, it was IT, and if it wasn't IT, it was accounting. The things that I didn't do well are genetically flawed in the whole business. I was not an accountant and had no interest in it. I had no interest or skill at IT or manufacturing. They became the weakest parts of the business. What I was really interested in as an artist was graphic design, which was a strong part of the business, and marketing and sales. Those were always stronger than manufacturing was. Sales would always outpace our ability to fulfill."

By 1993, Burt's Bees had realized the promise of its headquarters and actually become a general store of sorts. There were hundreds of products, all of them produced by hand. The business had reached $3 million in sales, an unimaginable climb from the $3,000 Burt had been doing on his own selling honey. Roxanne incorporated Burt's Bees, giving herself two-thirds of the ownership equity and Burt the other third. Burt didn't have the motivation that Roxanne did, and he really was not interested in either business or money. To Roxanne business was a game and she had already succeeded at it past her wildest dreams. It was increasingly clear to Quimby, however, that Maine was not the right state for the business as it expanded. "Burt's last big mission for Burt's Bees was to help scout out a location for the business in a state with a tax and regulatory environment more favorable to growth. He did a great job," Quimby adds. "He interviewed various state commerce departments and narrowed it down to a couple, and then narrowed it down further to N[orth]

C[arolina]. We went to NC and they took us around and showed us what they had to offer, and it was just what we needed, so we moved."

It was a wrenching transition. There were 44 employees, and she offered the seven most valuable ones free relocation to the new plant. Four agreed to come for a short period, but none moved permanently. Quimby also had not thought through the implications of recruiting highly educated workers, who make up a competitive labor pool. "Suddenly I'm hiring MBAs, and where I was paying $7 or $8 an hour for handwork in Maine—and that was a good job there—I had to pay $15 in North Carolina." This fundamental shift in its economics forced a reevaluation of the entire business. → salary change

It was at this moment that Quimby discovered the 80/20 rule. → cut a ton of products as a result "Twenty percent of our products were responsible for over 80 percent of our sales." Understanding this, and looking hard at the economics of handmade products in North Carolina, led Quimby to a very difficult decision: Burt's Bees would have to drop hand-dipped candles, honey, and many other lower-margin, labor-intensive products. It was a pivotal moment for the business. "I had this vision in my mind of a plant getting transplanted. When you're transplanting something that's growing and starting to get a foothold, you have to cut it back so it's not sending its vital energy out to the very tips of the branches, because you want it to go into the roots. So you cut it back and you transplant it. I thought of that process with the company. I was radically cutting it back so that it could take root in its new home, and recover from that pruning, and be all the stronger for it."

The pruning worked, and with results that exceeded Quimby's most optimistic forecasts. By 1995, Burt's Bees had eliminated candles and most other handmade items. The strength of the lip balm business allowed the company to invest in manufacturing equipment without taking loans. In 1999, Quimby bought out Burt, becoming the sole owner of Burt's Bees. By the year 2003, the $3 million business that Quimby had transplanted from Maine was making $60 million in revenues. The business had grown to over 200 employees, and Quimby realized that taking it to the next level would demand significant capital plus organizational skills of a sort that didn't match her strengths. She decided to sell.

sold to help it get to next level

As our lunch lingers into the afternoon at Walter's, Roxanne tells me about her initiation into the world of corporate finance. She was lucky enough to find an investment banker cut from her own cloth, a woman named Gail Zauder who had decided to go it on her own because she was not comfortable in the clubby male world of private equity. Quimby, who had never needed outside financing, quickly learned that private equity was a very special kingdom. And Zauder learned that Quimby didn't much like meeting with buyer after buyer, always repeating the same presentation for them. The meetings quickly jumbled together in Quimby's memory, making it impossible to discuss the advantages of one prospect over another. So Zauder devised a trick. She started calling ahead to each firm and telling them that Quimby was a finicky eater. She would ask for unusual gourmet food. Quimby may not have been finicky, but she certainly appreciated food. And she remembered the different meals and along with them the personalities of the financiers she met at each place.

The private equity world was unprepared for Quimby. "It was overwhelmingly male," she says. "At one place we were literally the only women in the room. I mean, they had to call a female assistant in to tell us where the women's bathroom was in their own office!" Quimby cared as much about character as money. She had built her business from scratch and wanted to place it in good hands. (She tells me at this point that her initial investment was $400 in supplies to repackage the honey, a sum that back then had struck her as immense.)

And Roxanne had some unusual ways of judging character. For one thing, she made a habit of bringing a deck of tarot cards to the meetings. She would choose a card for the head person at each firm. The results seemed to mirror her intuition. "I left $23 million on the table because I had a bad feeling about this one guy. He kept telling me that he was going to win, that he would pay whatever it took." So Roxanne pulled out her deck, and the card the man picked was the Devil. While I am sitting across the table from Quimby, momentarily stunned into silence at the thought of giving away $23 million because of a bad feeling and a Tarot card, she offers an explanation. "It's not just the money. You have to realize that you're getting into bed with these people. If there's no trust, then they'll find a way to screw you in the end. That money is an illusion because there's always ways they can make things go badly for you if they're not honorable."

The firm Quimby eventually chose (AEA Investors) was one where she saw eye-to-eye with the principal, Vincent Mai. Ironically, AEA also served the worst food, becoming known to Quimby and Zauder as the "worst lunch" place until AEA got wind and answered with a lavish spread at one of the later meetings. "We heard you think our food is terrible," an executive told the women. The agreed purchase price was $175 million, with $150 million coming in cash and the rest as retained equity in the company. Quimby continued to run Burt's Bees for a year during the transition, and then she took a seat on the board. She continues to like AEA and the firm's philosophy, although she has knocked heads with the chief marketing officer, a male ex-L'Oreal executive.

Six months after my visit with Quimby, AEA successfully sells Burt's Bees to the Clorox Corporation for $925 million in cash. In addition to quadrupling the value of the company, the sale will more than double Quimby's profit from the sale of Burt's Bees.

Quimby drives me back to the Portland airport, where I race to catch a flight earlier than the one I had booked. I barely make it on the plane, which turns out to be the last one leaving the airport that day. As we take off, the clouds part and the storm that has threatened all day descends on Portland.

Bangor is a city of contradictions. It has just over thirty thousand residents, making it half the size of Greenwich, Connecticut, yet it is the third largest city in Maine. It was the center of the logging business in Maine, which gave it a rough-and-tumble reputation but also made it one of the richest cities in the nineteenth-century United States. Bangor has the oldest symphony orchestra in the country, an opera house, and a large number of historic churches, yet it was also the site of one of the deadliest shootouts of the gangster era of the 1930s, when Al Brady of the Brady Gang, public enemy number one, was shot down by FBI agents in front of Dakin's Sporting Goods on Central Street. Bangor is 130 miles northeast of Portland and lies inland.

Although Roxanne Quimby owns four houses in Portland, it is in the hinterlands of Bangor that she first settled in Maine over 30 years ago. I arrive in Bangor two months after my visit to Portland for two reasons. Roxanne Quimby has offered to take me on a visit to some of the woods she is protecting near Baxter State Park. And she has put me in touch with Burt Shavitz, who after some cajoling has agreed to meet with me the next day. Roxanne is heading north from Bangor to survey some land she is considering purchasing on the eastern side of the Penobscot River, and she is on a timetable. If my flight doesn't land on time, she'll continue north without me and I'll be forced to rent a car and try to catch her en route. Fortunately, the commuter jet reaches Bangor early, and I'm waiting at the curb in front of the Bangor airport when a pickup truck pulls up and Roxanne's head pokes out of the passenger side door. "David!" she says with a smile. "Let's go!"

Roxanne is with her real estate agent. He is a calm man, and after 30 years of dealing with Maine's lumber barons, he has a keen sense of the politics of land. As I sit in the back seat of the extended cab pickup, the two discuss the land they'll be seeing. I begin to appreciate the finesse with which Quimby is piecing together the territory she is protecting. The real problem is that there's no single owner of the land she wants to buy. It's a patchwork of different plots, most of them used for logging, a scattered few for private homes or private recreation. Access poses a tangle of issues. Some of the plots have given right of ways (for road use) to specific companies to allow them to transport timber along the meager network of dirt and gravel roads. Then there are the hunters and the all-terrain vehicle enthusiasts and snowmobilers. These folks don't own any land or have legal right of way on the patches they traverse, but they do have a history of free access to it. Both hunters and snowmobilers are organized, and they make up a political force that can easily create problems if Quimby doesn't work with them. Instead of fighting all of these groups, Quimby has taken a very pragmatic business approach. She sometimes doesn't try directly buying a given piece of land she has her eye on. What she does is to buy a different plot entirely, one that she knows will have value to the owner of the first piece of land. Then she trades. Along the way, she negotiates hunting access and the right of way for snowmobile and ATV trails on the land she is swapping. At the time we meet, Quimby has been able to purchase 85,000 contiguous acres next to Baxter State Park and protect the land from development, logging, hunting, and all vehicular traffic.

About an hour north of Bangor, the landscape starts to change and we stop to get our first view of Mount Katahdin. It is a breathtaking peak, the second tallest in the eastern United States, and even on this early July day it seems to shimmer off in the mist, past a river and lush stands of trees. This part of Maine is still wild. There are roads and some houses, but the view has not changed much since Thoreau came to climb the mountain in 1846. We pile back into the pickup and after another half hour of driving stop at a Shell Station–cum-diner where we meet the rest of the team. This consists of Bart DeWolfe, who is Quimby's science director, along with DeWolfe's assistant, named Eric, and two interns, Sarah Stevens and Bryan Brown.

These folks are responsible for helping Quimby survey the property she is purchasing, and along the way they are recording the plant and animal species that they encounter. It's their job to understand the access points for each piece of land, and to figure out ways that the plots falling within the protected area can be sealed off from motorized access.

DeWolfe is an intelligent man, a Princeton and MIT graduate with Coke-bottle glasses and curly gray hair. Ecology is a second career for him, even though he got his Ph.D. in the field in the 1960s. He went on to a career as an aerospace engineer working on orbital navigation systems and took early retirement to change careers. Roxanne found him when he took an internship at the age of 60 mapping natural communities on the first two properties that she acquired. DeWolfe proved clever at detecting and documenting a plot's usage, and on one parcel was able to show that 1,200 snowmobiles had passed through in a month's time. Roxanne hired him to survey the land in subsequent properties, to look at erosion and conservation issues, and to help construct deals that would allow her to get the properties that she wanted.

Maine can be cold even in the middle of the summer, and we're all wearing fleeces as we chat outside the station. I walk inside with Roxanne to procure a few sandwiches for lunch. As she is standing in the middle of the store, a thickset man wearing a green work shirt and matching cap approaches her. "Are you Roxanne?" he asks. "Yup," she says, looking him in the eye. "Quimby?" he probes. "Yup," she responds. "Y'er a little far from home, aren't you," the man says, making it a statement. Not waiting for a reply, he turns on his heel and leaves the store. Roxanne is frozen for a moment and then, when he is out of sight, she laughs. Over at the register, the checkout woman turns to her and says, "If you ask me, I think you're right. I wouldn't let anybody on my property if I bought it either!"

For a woman with a good chance of being enshrined in Maine history as one of its great public benefactors, Quimby has an unusual talent for provoking controversy. This may be because she does not have a single political bone in her body. When Roxanne sees a problem, she wants to solve it in the most expedient manner possible. This tendency played out in Winter Harbor, where Roxanne keeps a summer house. Several years ago, Quimby purchased a half–burned-out apartment house in the center of town with two acres of land adjoining. She refurbished the apartment house and on the first floor opened up an Internet café, a feature she thought the town greatly needed. Winter Harbor is one of those quaint seaside Maine towns that attract a lot of tourists (in fact, the town sees about 250,000 a year), but it has no green space and no public restrooms. Quimby decided to turn her building's two acres of land into a town green. She would landscape the area, put down benches, and put in a bathroom for the public. Her feeling was that the look of the area would dramatically improve and land values would increase. Roxanne's first instinct was to put in the park as a fait accompli, but she yielded to advice suggesting that she should hold a town meeting. She was surprised when most residents of the town said they wanted the space to be a parking lot, which was a project she had no interest in doing. Then the *Portland Press Herald* wrote up the controversy in an article that repeatedly referred to Quimby as "Big Bucks" and labeled her an outsider. I ask her about this and she says, "There's a joke in Maine where a bunch of people attend a man's funeral. He lived in this Maine town for 70 years, since he was two years old. In the eulogy his friend says, 'He was almost one of us.'"

In the end, the townspeople perversely mobilized to prevent the construction of the town green. Quimby, disgusted, gave way. She has sold her Internet café and shelved her plans for a cooking school. (The zoning ordinance was denied.) In the end, the town will most likely get its parking lot, but the lot will be privately owned and the townspeople will pay to park there. Quimby doesn't suffer fools easily, and nothing seems so foolish to an entrepreneur as the mentality of a small town. Although it does amuse her. Quimby recently put out a rumor that she was selling her place and moving south, down the coast. "I do like a town where the rumor gets all the way back to you by sunset," she laughs.

Between the Winter Park controversy and her widespread land acquisition near Baxter, Quimby has become a lightning rod in the struggle between the old Maine and the new. If you drive around Maine long enough and watch closely, you'll see "Ban Roxanne" bumper stickers. Governor Baxter was fortunate to live in an age without bumpers.

As we drive through the woods near Baxter State Park, I realize how lucky it is that my flight did not arrive late. I would have been depending on a small GPS unit to allow me to find Quimby, and where we're traveling the unit in her pickup truck doesn't record any roads at all—the muddy, rutted path we're following does not qualify. The land parcels we're inspecting are under contract and Quimby hopes to close on them soon. They're on the wrong side of the Penobscot River for the park, but she plans to swap them for land she really wants, after constructing an agreement so that snowmobilers can maintain a route here after she trades the parcels away. The agreement, she hopes, will help win over snowmobiler groups—the clubs and organizations that snowmobilers join to organize group outings—so that the groups will use their influence to keep members away from the parcels of land Quimby does want to protect. Although DeWolfe and his crew do a good job of identifying where bridges can be taken down or barriers put in place, it is very difficult to seal off the Maine wilderness from small vehicles like snowmobiles and ATVs. The only hope is to persuade the groups to police their own members.

After tumbling along trails for several hours and eating lunch in the rain (the weather shifts dramatically from moment to moment, and we alternately get intense clear blue skies and sudden downpours), we stop at a piece of land that directly borders Baxter State Park. This is land that Quimby will keep, and she has already convinced the park's administration to remove a bridge spanning the creek between Baxter and her property. As the interns squat to examine foliage, Quimby, DeWolfe, and the developer huddle in a circle, discussing how best to return the site to the wild. Quimby suggests taking out the concrete bridge abutments, but DeWolfe says this may cause more environmental harm than good. In time the environment will cleanse itself, he says. We say goodbye and begin the slow drive back to Bangor.

The next morning, I'm nervously sitting in a gazebo by the river in Guilford. I am less than a mile away from the old bowling alley and general store where Burt's Bees was housed before it left Maine in 1993. The gazebo I am sitting in also has history for Burt's Bees. Neither Roxanne nor Burt liked working indoors all day, so they would make up excuses to get outside. When they interviewed candidates for Burt's Bees, the pair would conduct the interviews in this small gazebo, which has a nice view of the river and a small dam in the distance.

After about 15 minutes, Burt approaches cautiously with his rambunctious golden retriever. I like dogs, but it's difficult to take notes with a wet tongue in your face, so Burt ties off his leash while we talk. Burt is not what I expect. He does look like the guy on the tin of lip balm that I carry in my pocket, but he's a lot more neatly dressed than I expected. After all, this is a man who lives without electricity or running water. I ask him about the provenance of the various articles of clothing and accessories he's wearing, and I learn that there is a story behind each one. The hat, which to me looked like a fisherman's cap, is in fact a U.S. Army Ranger hat, purchased from army surplus. The frayed tan canvas boots are vintage Israeli Army desert boots—hard to find. His gray wool vest is a riding vest from Woolrich. He found the lavender Oxford he is wearing underneath the vest at a yard sale. His belt buckle is from the U.S. Cavalry, and his belt was hand tooled by a friend who is a harness maker.

Burt has conflicting feelings about journalists. He doesn't want me to record our interview, but he is perfectly content waiting while I scribble copious notes and ask him to repeat himself. He is suspicious about meeting me and insists that we meet in a public place in broad daylight (which is fine with me, too), but he soon offers to show me his camp if I have time. Yet every time I ask a question that seems too personal, he stops, scowls, and asks me more questions about my book, my publisher, and what I am writing about.

Burt Shavitz was born at Doctor's Hospital (since razed) in the Yorkville neighborhood of New York City, and he grew up in Flushing, Queens, and in nearby Great Neck, Long Island. By his own account, he didn't fit in at school and he particularly disliked being cooped up inside a schoolroom. After high school, Shavitz spent two years attending college out of state, then quit and returned home. He was drafted and served for two years with the U.S. Army's Third

Infantry Division at Fort Benning, Georgia, and in Germany. In the army, Shavitz served in the line infantry and drove a jeep with an antitank gun, ending up as a battalion photographer for the Third Medical Battalion. Back in the States, Shavitz attended photography school while living with his parents, who had moved into Manhattan. Then he rented a darkroom and worked steadily as a photographer's assistant while he tried to get freelance jobs as a photojournalist.

Burt got an early break with an assignment from a lay Catholic magazine to document a community of Lubavitchers in New York City's Williamsburg neighborhood. As he built his portfolio, his stark, honest style won him progressively more serious jobs. By the early 1960s, he was a stringer for Time Life. He took the centerfold photo for the first Earth Day in *Life* magazine, and a picture of the Statue of Liberty rising from a pile of garbage that became a rallying image for the nascent environmental movement. Shavitz also covered politics. He took pictures of Roy Cohn at the McCarthy hearings and some of the biggest names of the day. Among his most dramatic pictures are his portraits of Malcom X, which can still be viewed in the Time Life archives. Shavitz almost always photographed Malcolm X from below and at an angle. His photos capture the presence and the drama of Malcolm X in life, and the turbulent emotions at his funeral.

The photojournalist role kept Shavitz in New York City and despite his success, he was increasingly unhappy in the urban environment. In 1970, he received a grant from the New York State Council on the Arts for a creative project that allowed him to move out of the city to Ulster County. He never moved back and never returned to photojournalism. Instead, Burt took a series of jobs that allowed him to work less and increasingly put him further into the wilderness. His first spot was as a caretaker for a cottage on the lake at Mohonk Mountain House in New Paltz, New York. He also worked setting type for some time, and eventually he met a man who kept bees. Burt had heard that beekeeping could make you a living without eating up too much time. He apprenticed with two different beekeepers to learn the craft. Shavitz also learned how to get bees out of buildings, making money from bee removal while providing him with a source of free bees for his own hives. He spent a decade keeping bees in Ulster County before property values rose to the point where he had to move out. He headed north to Maine, for largely the same reasons that Roxanne would several years later.

Burt was always a recluse, and Maine seemed to enhance his natural inclinations. Burt bought a little bit of land and built his own camp (which, in Maine, is a term referring to any living arrangement you construct by hand, whether it is a tent in an open field, a cabin, or a crudely built house). At the time he met Quimby, Burt was selling his bees' honey in the parking lot of a machine shop in Dexter that served a fish peddler, a farmer, and a few other merchants as the site of a spontaneous flea market on the weekends.

I ask Burt about Quimby, and his admiration and disapproval for her life register at equal levels. "She had more energy than a bullet from a pistol," he says, but it is not entirely a compliment. Burt admits that he was never interested in building a business and was happy to retire when Quimby moved Burt's Bees to North Carolina. He still maintains a connection to the company that bears his name, and they use him at PR events, as Roxanne did when she was the CEO. In fact, Burt has just returned from North Carolina, where he has participated in a company event that sounds more like a revival meeting (complete with a large tent) than a picnic. The CEO had Shavitz ride in on a Harley, and the two of them drummed together under the tent. The event raised the emotions of employees to a fever pitch, and some were weeping before it was over.

Burt has exactly the life he wants. At 72, he's free to spend an hour grooming his dog or a day figuring out how to fix his lawnmower. As we finish our talk, I follow him in his old Mercedes station wagon out of Guilford to Parkman, where he still lives on the land that Roxanne owns. His camp is in fact a small, two-story structure with a potbellied stove and total interior volume that can't be more than 300 square feet. Just up the hill, empty, is the house that Roxanne lived in for 13 years. It, too, started as a modest cabin, but Quimby eventually added rooms and conveniences. Even so, by the time she moved out the former cabin was still just a two-bedroom house, smaller than the living room of her Baxter house, and she was the CEO of a $30 million company. When I talk to Roxanne about her old home, and the tent where she lived when she first met Burt, she says, "That's what I need to do. I should live in a tent this summer. Maybe that's why I don't feel at home anywhere. I just need to simplify."

AFTERWORD

Every brand begins with a story and ends with a promise. Whether you are an entrepreneur or a big-company marketer, it's important to remember to tell the story and honor that promise. If you have started your own business, you certainly have a sense of this already. You've found yourself writing e-mails at 2:00 A.M., scouting your warehouse on Saturday morning, or checking twice with FedEx to ensure that an important package was received. Pretty soon, though, there will be too many customers for you to know each one individually, and you'll have to call them consumers. That's when you had better understand the promise that your brand is making and ensure the rest of your crew knows it too.

I have read that elite athletes and musicians are not necessarily physically more gifted than good amateurs. Instead, they have mastered the art of practice. When elite athletes practice, they start by analyzing their own weaknesses and then make small adjustments. Once they've found a way to become even a little bit better, they train their muscles to remember the way they did it. I believe that successful entrepreneurs develop the same sort of talent. When most of us make mistakes, we get upset, we brood, and, if we are mature, we apologize to those around us and move on. The best entrepreneurs take an additional step. They think through their errors, and then think around them. They mentally work through how they will avoid making the same mistake the next time. These folks don't do this because they've taken a workshop, read a book, or studied Six Sigma. They do it because mistakes cost them money, hurt them personally, and threaten their families. Every good entrepreneur I have ever met feels like the wolf is just outside the door, no matter how successful his or her business.

This is a good thing to remember if you're reading this book while secure in the bosom of a great corporation. There is a good chance that you're competing with somebody who regards success as a life-and-death matter. That's the brand you want to watch out for. Not just because they make decisions faster than you do, but also because they sweat the details. They understand the customer in a way you don't. They have targeted you as the enemy and all of their loyal customers know why. They know how to tell their own story so customers will repeat it. They won't forget those customers as their business grows. And they are not going to give up easily, not at all.

This book has been a short tour of a vast landscape. Although the media focuses most of its attention on Fortune 500 companies, small businesses play a vital role in the fabric of the U.S. economy. According to the Small Business Administration, not only do small businesses (those with fewer than 500 employees) generate 60 percent to 80 percent of all new jobs, they create more than half of the private gross domestic product (GDP) in the United States. Perhaps even more important, small businesses produce 14 times more patents than large firms and the patents they produce are twice as likely to be cited. Look at the pharmaceutical and biotech industries (as well as other industries), and you'll see that most of the exciting, dynamic work is being done by small companies started by folks just like you. The entire fabric of our daily life would come apart if individuals did not have the courage to abandon the security of a steady paycheck for the promise of building their own business.

Moreover, don't be too glum about your prospects as an entrepreneur. A recent study suggests that despite the myth that 90 percent of new businesses fail in the first year, nearly half of small businesses survive for at least four years [Knaup, Amy E. "Survival and Longevity in the Business Employment Dynamics Database." *Monthly Labor Review*, 8.5 (2005)]. If you can survive for four years, chances are you've figured out how to make money. To thrive, you just need to learn to take the next step, which is to become indispensable to your customers.

My last word of advice is to remember that you are not alone. There are other entrepreneurs all around you who are experiencing the same challenges and frustrations. Your local chamber of commerce, Rotary Club, continuing education program, or business networking group may be a great place to get ideas and support. Moreover, there are a lot of successful men and women running midsize to large companies who were once in exactly the same spot as you, and many would be happy to help you. Gary Erickson reached out to Yves Chouinard (at Patagonia) and Mo Siegel (who founded Celestial Seasonings) for advice when he decided not to sell his company. Don't be afraid to pick up the phone or send an e-mail and ask for advice. And don't forget to return the favor when you become successful. Good luck to you.

INDEX